MW00628353

Regaining Your Spiritual Momentum

DAVE WILLIAMS

Regaining Your Spiritual Momentum

DAVE WILLIAMS

Regaining Your Spiritual Momentum

ISBN   0-938020-65-X

First Printing 2002

Cover Design: Beverly Woodard &
Gerard R. Jones

Published by

DECAPOLIS
PUBLISHING
Printed in the United States Of America

BOOKS BY DAVE WILLIAMS

ABCs of Success and Happiness
The AIDS Plague
The Art Of Pacesetting Leadership
The Beauty of Holiness
Christian Job Hunter's Handbook
The Desires of Your Heart
Depression, Cave of Torment
Filled
Genuine Prosperity, The Power To Get Wealth
Getting To Know Your Heavenly Father
Gifts That Shape Your Life And Change Your World
The Grand Finale Revival
Grief and Mourning
Growing Up in Our Father's Family
Have You Heard From the Lord Lately?
How to Be a High Performance Believer
The Jezebel Spirit
Laying On of Hands
Lonely in the Midst of a Crowd
The Miracle Results of Fasting
The New Life . . . The Start of Something Wonderful
The Pastor's Pay
Patient Determination
Revival Power of Music
Remedy for Worry and Tension
The Road To Radical Riches
The Secret of Power With God
Seven Signposts on the Road to Spiritual Maturity
Slain in the Spirit — Real or Fake?
Somebody Out There Needs You
Success Principles From the Lips of Jesus
Supernatural Soulwinning
Thirty-Six Minutes with the Pastor
Understanding Spiritual Gifts
What To Do If You Miss The Rapture
The World Beyond — The Mysteries of Heaven
Your Pastor: A Key To Your Personal Wealth

Contents

*Success is reaching the
end of the line and knowing
we did our best for God in
the time allotted to us
on earth.*

First Thoughts

The Road To Success

The longest street in the world is called Yonge Street, and begins in Toronto, Canada, then stretches nearly 1,200 miles west along the U.S.-Canada border, not far north of where I live.

There are lots of roads in the world, and few of them garner that kind of fame. Most roads are a few miles long, and some are just a few hundred feet long. Some are important and are kept up by the city or county; others are in disrepair and seem to have outlived their usefulness. Old Route 66, stretching from Chicago to Los Angeles, used to be a bustling thoroughfare, and even had a popular song written about it. But when a modern highway was built alongside it, Route 66 began to deteriorate and now is home mostly to shady motels and trinket shops. People only drive on it for nostalgia's sake, and some parts are even overgrown with grass.

It is important to know where a road will take you before you embark on it. Roads are a good metaphor for life because each of us is on a road heading somewhere. If we are believers in Christ, we are on the road God has marked out for us — the road of destiny, joy and success. If we are not believers, we are headed on a road that will end abruptly and with terrifying results. If you have started reading this book and you do not know Christ, I invite you to turn to page 181 at the back of the book and read more about the new life you can have starting right now.

Every road has its perils, even for those of us who follow Christ. At times we might:

- find ourselves on the Road of Troubles.

- get a flat tire.

- run out of gas.

- drift over the center line.

- make a wrong turn.

- be drawn away from our destination by a flashy roadside attraction.

- lose our motivation for staying on the right road.

- wind up on the reprobate road.

This book is about how to stay on the Road to Success. By "success" I mean living a life that pleases God, serving Him in every possible way. For the follower of Christ, success is what Paul referred to in Galatians:

> **I have been crucified with Christ and I no longer live, but Christ lives in me.**
>
> **—Galatians 2:20a**

Success is reaching the end of the line and knowing we did our best for God in the time allotted to us on earth. We will talk about the pitfalls, big and small, that can take us off the Road to Success, and how we can get back on it again. These pages are full of life-changing truths that will equip you for the journey to genuine success.

Maybe some day you will visit Yonge Street or Route 66; but even if you don't, you can embark on the Road to Success. Travel with me now as we discover road-tested truths from the Word of God, and arrive safely at our place of destiny. Let's go!

Fear speeds us down the road of trouble; faith helps us to turn around and head the other way.

Chapter One

The Road Of Trouble

If you are alive, you know what trouble is. We are not in this world for thirty seconds before we encounter a problem. "I'm hungry" is our first trouble. From then on we have one after another.

"I'm sleepy."

"I'm sick."

"I need braces."

"I blew a test."

"I need to go to college."

"I need a job."

"I need a place to retire."

To be troubled is to be disturbed, agitated, harassed, and in pain or discomfort. In the biblical languages, the word for trouble means a narrow, tight place, to stir or agitate, to crowd in. Trouble is the fly in the ointment, the monkey wrench in the works. Trouble is when you lose your glasses but can't look for them until you find them.

A boy came home and said to his mom and dad, "There is a small PTA meeting at the school tonight we need to go to." His mother said, "If it is just a small meeting, I don't think we'll go." The boy said, "You have to. It is with you, Dad, the principal, and me."

I am amazed at how many people I know who face trouble. Money trouble, relationship trouble, school trouble, job trouble, car trouble, health trouble. What to do? God has direction for people when they are facing trouble, and in this chapter I am going to show you the road map out of trouble.

But where does trouble come from? It can come from three general directions: the devil, other people, or ourselves. The Bible says the devil sent a messenger, or demon, to trouble Paul everywhere he went, and other people, as we all know, can cause lots of trouble in our lives.

Many of our troubles however, come from ourselves and from a lack of knowledge.

Hosea said:

> My people are destroyed from lack of knowledge.
>
> —Hosea 4:6a

Knowledge is power to overcome trouble. I heard an awful story about a man who hated his wife's cat. She went to visit her sister for two days and he took the cat by the scruff of the neck and drowned it. When she got home he said, "Honey, your cat is gone." She said, "I have got to find him. I love that cat." The husband comforted her and said, "I will put an ad in the newspaper advertising a one thousand dollar reward for anyone who returns it." When a friend learned about the reward, he said, "That is a lot of money to pay for a cat." The husband said, "Not if you know what I know."

Knowledge can give you power, but lack of knowledge keeps us from power.

Take health, for example. We have all heard stories of people in centuries past who died when the expert doctors of the day tried weird methods to cure them of illnesses. Doctors used to believe that bleeding a patient made him healthier, but now we know that bleeding speeds people toward death. As knowledge has increased in the medical field, so has the survival rate.

A doctor I know of told how a lady came to him weighing more than three hundred pounds. She said she was having heart and arthritis problems, so the doctor asked about her diet, and she said, "For every meal I eat from all the food groups. When I go to McDonald's I have a big hamburger and get my meat and grain. I eat French fries to get my starch and, of course, there is a tomato and lettuce on the burger so I get my vegetables. I have a milk shake to get my dairy group, and an apple pie for my fruit group." He asked what she ate at home and she said, "I am a steak and potatoes woman. I like to have steak every night to get my iron and protein. I have a potato to get my starch and I put sour cream on it for the dairy group. When I am ready to get my fruit group I have a Key Lime pie."

She was absolutely sincere, and believed she should be healthy. Her real trouble was lack of knowledge.

Taking The Correct Turns

Even when we have the right knowledge, trouble can come our way. What do we do when we face it? We can learn from a famous example — the children of Israel. They had been abused for centuries, enslaved by Egyptians who demanded more of them than anyone could reasonably give. The children of

Israel cried out to God in their trouble, and God raised up a deliverer named Moses who told Pharaoh, the king, to let God's people go. Pharaoh refused, so God through Moses worked miracles of judgment on Egypt. Lice, frogs, water turned to blood, flies, a plague on livestock, hail, locusts, gnats, boils, darkness and the final plague when the first born died in every home without blood on the doorposts. By that time, the Egyptians were so happy to see them go that they basically plundered themselves and sent the wealth of Egypt with them.

But the Israelites had trouble ahead. They came to the Red Sea and could not go any farther, and then the Egyptian army approached because Pharaoh had changed his mind.

The five turns they took next give us a roadmap out of trouble. We are going to talk about specific troubles in the coming chapters, but these principles provide the broad foundation for getting out of any troublesome situation. I challenge you to take these same turns any time you face a bad situation, and watch how God works on your behalf.

Turn Number One: Cry out to God.

When we are desperate for God's intervention, we are near to our answer. I spoke with a new convert recently. He told me that the week after he accepted Jesus he faced all sorts of temptations, but that he cried out to Jesus and was spared all of them.

Crying out shows that our hearts are sincere. It is a humbling experience. We should forget about dignity when we need direction.

I think of the woman in the Gospels who had a hemorrhage, probably from leukemia. Over the course of twelve years she had spent much money on doctors, but had not stopped bleeding. Then she heard about Jesus and dragged herself out of the house to find Him. When she saw the crowd pressing in around Him, she was not discouraged. She did not say, "It must not be God's will for me to reach Jesus." She got down on the ground and reached for Him, power went into her, and she was healed.

Have you ever felt that if you did not connect with God, you would die? Have you gone into your bedroom after a hard day, fallen on the bed and literally cried out in prayer? I have. It is called reaching the end of your rope, and it is where God begins to lead us out of trouble.

Turn Number Two: Do not fear.

Moses told the people, "Fear ye, not." In the New Testament, James 1:2 says, "Count it pure joy whenever you face trials of many kinds." Why? Because it is an opportunity for God to give you a miracle. Fear speeds us down the Road of Trouble; faith helps us to turn around and head the other way.

Turn Number Three: Stand still.

There are times when trouble will stare us in the face like a tiger out of its cage, and we will need to simply stand still and wait for instructions.

> Moses answered the people, "Do not be afraid. Stand firm and you will see the deliverance the LORD will bring you today. The Egyptians you see today you will never see again. The LORD will fight for you; you need only to be still."
>
> —Exodus 14:13-14

Have you ever panicked and made a bad situation worse? That is what God was teaching them not to do. I am sure there were plenty of opinions about what action to take in the face of the Egyptian threat.

- Meet them in battle?

- Hide in the wilderness?

- Swim for it?

But God instructed them to stand still and to wait for the right answer.

The answer to put you on the path away from trouble may come through a pastor's sermon, an evangelist on television, a book, a radio program, or during your daily Bible devotion, but God *will* give you a word on what to do. His Word to Moses was to tell the people to stand still and not do anything until God gave further instructions. Then He told Moses what to do, and the man of God stretched forth his hand, and the people walked through on dry ground. No other solution would have saved them, and they may have gotten into worse trouble if they had not stood still and waited.

Turn Number Four: Follow the word of instruction.

God told the children of Israel to move ahead.

> And Moses stretched out his hand over the sea; and the LORD caused the sea to go *back* by a strong east wind all that night, and made the sea dry *land,* and the waters were divided. And the children of Israel went into the midst of the sea upon the dry *ground:* and the waters *were* a wall unto them on their right hand, and on their left.
>
> —Exodus 14:21-22 (KJV)

When God presents a solution, take it! Act on it! Do not delay!

Not only will God deliver you, He will vanquish your enemies. Paul says it is the Father's good pleasure to give tribulation to those who trouble you.

> Seeing *it is* a righteous thing with God to recompense tribulation to them that trouble you;
>
> —2 Thessalonians 1:6 (KJV)

When somebody troubles a child of God, look out — they just sabotaged their own life! The Egyptians found that out when they tried to pile onto God's miracle by taking the path through the sea. All of a sudden, the chariot wheels fell off and there was a mass pile-up, much worse than any car accident you have seen on the evening news. The next time the children of Israel saw the Egyptians was when their bodies were washing up on the shore. Why? Because God counts it a pleasure to cause tribulation to come to those who trouble his people.

> The water flowed back and covered the chariots and horsemen — the entire army of Pharaoh that had followed the Israelites into the sea. Not one of them survived... That day the Lord saved Israel from the hands of the Egyptians, and Israel saw the Egyptians lying dead on the shore.
>
> —Exodus 14:28, 30

Turn Number Five: Look for your miracle.

This almost goes without saying, but God will continue to provide miracles when you sincerely want to leave the Road of Trouble and head back to the Road to Success. This whole journey we are on will be full of miracles, big and small. Each morning we should wake up expecting a miracle, whether it is help out of a financial scrape, help in a relational matter, or even the fact that we can take the next breath. Life is a series of miracles that we may or may not recognize, and God's goodness is in each one.

Are you on the Road of Trouble? It is no shame. Many are the afflictions of the righteous, but the Lord will deliver us from them all. This entire book is about getting off a Road of Trouble of one kind or another. And as we will see in the next chapter, sometimes our way back to the Road to Success will be by a very unexpected route.

Chapter Two

Becoming A Trouble Untangler

The woman stands next to her car along the busy highway, her hood up, engine steaming, the sun beating down on her.

"If only I had my cell phone with me," she thinks as the eighteen-wheelers and sedans whip by. "Now I'm stranded, and nobody is stopping to help."

A chill runs down her spine as she imagines some shady character pulling over, teeth missing, greasy clothes and a salacious grin sneering at her as he opens his door and walks over to her, and she prays harder, "Please, God, let someone nice stop to help me get my car going, or at least let them lend me a phone to call a tow truck."

The minutes pass and dozens of drivers go by without even looking her way.

"She'll get help," one man thinks. "I'm in a hurry."

"I don't trust people who stop along the highway," a woman thinks. "I bet it's a scam."

"I would stop, but I saw her too late and I don't want to turn around," thinks another man.

The woman is trapped, the car blinkers on, the engine still hissing, and after half an hour she decides she has no choice but to walk to the next exit, ten miles away. She leaves the car behind, stepping carefully with her high heel shoes.

"Forget the job interview," she says, looking at her watch. "Now it is just time to survive."

The road seems so long now that she is on foot and discouragement sets in. She begins to cry, her tears dropping to the asphalt, leaving a temporary trail behind her. In her mind she cannot silence the question that hurts her so much, "Why didn't anyone stop to help?"

Trouble Untanglers

If that scene has never happened to you, consider yourself blessed. Everybody has troubles. Nearly all of us can point to times in our past when we ran out of gas, overheated the engine or blew a critical part, and found ourselves suddenly as a road-side observer wishing somebody's good will would cause them to pull over.

We have all been in trouble in other areas of life, from marriage problems to an unfortunate financial situation, to teenagers driving us out of our minds. We have longed for someone with experience to acknowledge our plight, pull over, and help us.

Yet, why is it that we go to great lengths to get ourselves off the Road of Trouble, but use a much higher standard when deciding to help others? We need to help others out of trouble, too. We need to become trouble untanglers.

The world is full of messes, like balls of yarn that have been strung up in knots. You and I see people every day who, figuratively speaking, are tied hand and foot, or who are stranded on the side of the road of life wondering if someone will stop to help them.

As believers we have a duty to help troubled people, just as Jesus did. When He opened the scroll in the synagogue He quoted Isaiah 61:

> "The Spirit of the Lord is on me, because he has anointed me to preach good news to the poor. He has sent me to proclaim freedom for the prisoners and recovery of sight for the blind, to release the oppressed, to proclaim the year of the Lord's favor."
>
> —Luke 4:18,19

He was saying the Spirit of the Lord was upon Him to untangle people's troubles. Jesus paid the price to do that. He is the great Trouble Untangler. The Bible says that for this cause was the Son of God manifest that he might destroy the works of the devil. The word "destroy" in Greek means untangle.

I am quite convinced that some people remain ill, or troubled, because they are consumed with untangling their own troubles. If they untangled other people's troubles, God would untangle theirs!

> "Do not withhold good from those who deserve it, when it is in your power to act."
>
> —Proverb 3:27

God has given us that power. You and I were created to untangle somebody's trouble. When God created Adam he was in trouble for the same reason every man is in trouble before he has a woman. He was missing something and he did not know what. Eve helped untangle that trouble — his need for companionship.

Everything God created was to solve a problem or untangle a trouble. He created ears to solve the problem of hearing, eyes to solve the problem of seeing, legs to solve the problem of immobility.

And He has given us His Spirit so we will become trouble untanglers.

The Trouble With Money

Before God promotes you, He will weigh your contribution in untangling troubles of others. Take employers, for example. As an employee do you:

• look for ways to solve problems above and beyond what is expected of you?

• try to make your boss look good by working hard?

• honor your time commitment by arriving on time, leaving on time and not slacking off during the day?

Each of these things helps us untangle troubles. God will judge you by how you treat your employer, even if he is the nastiest guy in the world. Your worth to your boss is determined by how well you untangle problems for him or her, and if you are not untangling troubles for your boss, it is a good bet that you are dead weight or causing trouble.

When you untangle somebody's problems, God untangles your troubles. When I first entered the ministry, I decided I needed a new set of clothes, so I went to J.C. Penney and bought ties and a shirt. There was just one problem.

I had no idea how I was going to pay the bill.

The clothes cost around a hundred and fifty dollars, but it might as well have been ten thousand. The bill arrived in my mailbox like an unwelcome guest, and hung around my house as if taunting me.

"You'll never pay me off! Ha ha ha! I'll be here the rest of your life, long after they boot you out of that church," it seemed to say.

Then I received a letter from Rex Humbard, who was pastoring at the Cathedral of Tomorrow. I was on his list of supporters, so I opened the letter and began to read. Its theme was "I am In Trouble." The Securities Exchange Commission was after his church for issuing bonds without a prospectus, something churches have been doing for centuries. To untangle the trouble, Humbard had to pay the bonds off, and he said that if everybody who received this letter would send twenty-five dollars, it would be solved.

I finished the letter, set it down and shook my head.

"There he goes, begging for money," I thought, the J.C. Penney bill lingering in the back of my mind. "Doesn't he know there are ministers out here barely making ends meet?"

Not many days later I was walking to work one morning and the Lord said to me, "Dave, if you had that trouble and it was in somebody else's power to help you out of it, what would you want them to do?" I said, "I would want them to help me." He said, "I want you to help Rex out of his trouble, and I am going to help you out of yours."

I realized I had judged Rex because of my own financial difficulty, so I sent twenty-five dollars to Rex Humbard, and so did many others, enough to get him out of the trouble. Unfortunately, the J.C. Penney bill did not disappear, and the deadline for payment was drawing closer. About that time, I found a Scripture that intrigued me though I did not know exactly what it meant.

> ...Whatever you bind on earth will be bound in heaven, and whatever you loose on earth will be loosed in heaven.
>
> —Matthew 16:19b

I could hardly pray because my mind was consumed with worry about the bill. I went into my bedroom and said, "Lord, I do not know what binding and loosing means, but I am going to try it. Devil, I bind you in the name of Jesus, and Lord I ask you to loose angels on my behalf."

Suddenly the darkness was gone and the noonday sun shone in that bedroom. I walked out full of faith. Later that week I went to the mailbox and found an envelope containing four, fifty dollar bills. I had not told a soul except my wife about the department store bill, and to this day I have no idea who put the envelope in the mailbox, but I give the glory to God. He taught me a lesson about helping others, and then ran that bill right out of my house!

Finding Your Expertise

It is important to understand that you and I cannot untangle everybody's trouble. You should not pull off the side of the road to help everybody who is in trouble because you may not have the skills, and God may have someone coming along behind you who can get the job done quicker.

No one person has the power to untangle everybody's troubles, but each of us has the power to untangle somebody's troubles. We need to discover our area of expertise. Lawyers untangle legal troubles, but not everybody is called to be a lawyer. Mechanics untangle car troubles, car dealers untangle transportation troubles, physicians untangle health troubles. Everybody has a call, a destiny, a ministry of untangling troubles, but no one person can untangle them all. A surgeon may be skillful with the fine muscles in the heart, but be totally incapable of changing his car's oil.

I was driving through a city in Oklahoma some years back when a man ran a red light and broadsided my car, spinning me through the intersection and riddling my body with bruises and injuries. I was hospitalized and told I had to undergo physical therapy. Anyone who has been in a car accident knows what an awful, frightening experience it is, and I was shaken up emotionally and physically.

I returned to my home in Lansing and filled out the proper paperwork to report the claim to my insurance company, who I had been with for many years. Getting back in the swing of things took a few days, and I went through ups and downs, but I was comforted knowing that the accident was not my fault and that God had spared me any incapacitating injury.

Then I looked through the mail one day and saw a letter from my insurance company. I opened the envelope and was absolutely shocked when I saw that they had sent back my claim with a bold red stamp that read, "DENIED."

"Denied!" I thought. "How can they do that? Are they trying to tell me it was my fault?"

I called and wrote to them, but continued to receive paperwork and medical bills back with the big red stamp on them, meaning that I had to pay for every cost associated with my hospitalization and recovery. I was furious, feeling wrongly accused by my own insurance company of being a fraud, and feeling the weight of the medical bills. At night I would fume and worry, and every time I felt the pain of a bruise or injury I thought about how unfair the situation had become. I tried not to complain publicly, but the friends who knew about it could only shake their heads in sympathy, powerless to help.

After a few months of this, a man made an appointment to see me. He was a vice president for another insurance company and had heard about what I was going through, and on the day of the appointment he stormed into my office and said, "I am sick and tired of insurance companies like this one giving the insurance industry a black eye. Give me your paperwork and I am going to take care of it." Within days he resolved the matter entirely so that my bills were paid and the burden of responsibility was lifted. I was free to recover without having to think about doing battle with a big company.

I felt like jumping up and down and shouting, "Hallelujah!"

Out of nowhere, a man showed up who had the skills to help me, and he untangled my insurance troubles in a flash. He did what no one else I knew was capable of doing. Needless to say, I returned the favor and switched my insurance to his company immediately, and to this day I am grateful that he turned that situation around.

Gaining God's Blessing

Trouble untanglers are appreciated, loved, and respected, and to make it even better, they receive God's greatest blessings.

> Is not this the kind of fasting I have chosen: to loose the chains of injustice and untie the cords of the yoke, to set the oppressed free and break every yoke? Is it not to share your food with the hungry and to provide the poor wanderer with shelter — when you see the naked, to clothe him, and not to turn away from your own flesh and blood? Then your light will break forth like the dawn, and your healing will quickly appear; then your righteousness will go before you, and the glory of the LORD will be your rear guard.
>
> Then you will call and the LORD will answer; you will cry for help, and he will say: Here am I. If you do away with the yoke of oppression, with the pointing finger and malicious talk, and if you spend yourselves in behalf of the hungry and satisfy the needs of the oppressed, then your light will rise in the darkness, and your night will become like the noonday.
>
> The LORD will guide you always; he will satisfy your needs in a sun-scorched land and will strengthen your frame. You will be like a well-watered garden, like a spring whose waters never fail. Your people will rebuild the ancient ruins and will raise up the age-old foundations; you will be called Repairer of Broken Walls, Restorer of Streets with Dwellings.
>
> —Isaiah 58:6-12

God promises that if we untangle problems for other people, He will untangle ours. Look at all the promises in that passage:

- He will cause our light to break forth like the dawn by putting His glory on us.
- He will heal us.
- Our reputation of righteousness will precede us.
- He will protect us from trouble.
- He will answer us quickly.
- Even our dark times will be good, and the roughest day of our lives will be bright.
- He will guide us.
- He will provide for us.
- He will give us strong bodies.
- We will be prosperous.
- We will accomplish great things and be hailed as heroes.

If you are on the Road of Trouble, help someone else and watch how quickly God points you back in the right direction.

Chapter Three

Spiritual Momentum

There is another danger on the Road to Success, and it affects many Christians. Some call it burnout. I call it losing your spiritual momentum.

I was coming back from Africa after a missions crusade some years ago. We had rented an arena there, and during the meetings the power of God manifested in astonishing ways. God spoke to me with such clarity while I preached, and I called out the words God gave me and miracles happened in the congregation. When I gave the altar call, hundreds left their seats and came forward to receive Christ.

I boarded the international flight that would take me back to Michigan after this great Gospel campaign, settled into my seat and began to reflect on the wonderful things God had done. As I did, exhaustion set in and all the hard-driving, low-sleep weeks

I had spent caught up with me. My body and mind began to let down, and immediately I had another visitor aside from the men I was traveling with.

"You are such a failure," the voice told me. I reclined my seat and tried to ignore it, but it kept speaking.

"Look at you! Thirty-seven years old and this is the best you can do? A couple of puny services in Africa? Other men draw hundreds of thousands, but not you."

I slipped on headphones and listened to music over the airline system, but the voice kept nagging me, and it knew just where I felt weakest.

"And that little church of yours is not nearly as big and influential as you dreamed it would be. You can only draw a couple of thousand people while the rest of the city stays home and sleeps! You are not much of a pastor. Think of how many times you failed people, missed the mark, didn't do what you knew you should."

The plane ascended to cruising altitude over the Atlantic Ocean and my seatmates chatted and joked with each other, but I felt alone and vulnerable. Thoughts flew through my head like bats in the night sky, and though they had no real connection with reality I was consumed with disappointment. I had the most beautiful family anybody could ever want, the best church I could ask for and success far beyond what I deserved, but it seemed like I was locked in a dungeon.

My "up" attitude was gone, and so was my motivation.

Fourteen hours later we stepped onto American soil, and I wish I could say that I left those thoughts on the airplane, but the devil was not going to give up, and over the next few months, and even years, I was dogged by a feeling of failure. Though my family and the church kept growing, all was not well in the corridors of my heart. The devil was having a field day with me and all I could do was wonder why I seemed so powerless against the attacks.

My heart seemed cold.

Thank God I met a man who knew what I was going through. He was a leader in my church denomination and had studied burn-out for ten years. We had lunch together, and I listened to every word he spoke.

"What you are going through is not uncommon, Dave," he said. "Men burn out in the ministry every day. Interestingly, we did not lose any ministers in their sixties or twenties. All of them were in their thirties and forties, and almost all of them have been in the ministry for twelve years or more."

I realized then and there that I was going through what thousands of other men go through, and what King David went through. I had lost my spiritual momentum. David's battles were one right after another. Relentless. He seemed to get victory over one foe and another would pop up.

> Once again there was a battle between the Philistines and Israel. David went down with his men to fight against the Philistines, and he became exhausted.
>
> **—2 Samuel 21:15**

He got weary and lost his momentum; his energy began to wane; he grew tired of the things that harassed him.

It happens — but it does not *have* to happen. God put us on an exciting, adventurous Road to Success in this Christian life, and we do not need to lose our spiritual momentum, at least not for long.

The Long Journey

Most of us remember that excitement of coming to Christ, learning about being filled with the Holy Spirit, discovering our gifts, our ministry, learning about giving and receiving, about prayer.

Then the years go on and you face a battle, a challenge, a temptation or a trial. Unhealthy thoughts come to you and you slowly begin to believe them. Those are the very thoughts that will lead you into a ditch.

All along this Christian life you can see people in the ditch, who got off on the wrong exit and cannot seem to find their way back onto the highway. You see people stalled, out of gas, being distracted by the attractions on the side of the road.

I recently watched video footage of church services at our church taken a decade ago. As the camera panned the crowd, my wife Mary Jo and I saw many people we had not seen for years, and we began to ask each other, "Where did so-and-so go?" Sad to say, many had gone off on a wrong exit, run into a ditch or been distracted by attractions on the side of the road.

That is what happened to David when he grew weak. Our journey with Christ can become wearisome if we listen to the lies of the devil instead of listening to the facts of God's Word.

Mary Jo and the kids and I climbed in the car and got ready to head home after spending a few days in Tulsa. We were buoyant after our pleasant stay, and all of us looked forward to the trip back to Michigan.

We decided to drive a little bit, then find a hotel where we could spend the evening, enjoying a nice dinner, relaxing on the beds, perhaps swimming in the pool. The plan seemed perfect as we pulled onto the highway.

And then Mary Jo counted the money.

We had decided we were going to live debt free, and had cut up our credit cards a few months earlier so we would use cash only. Now we found ourselves with eighteen dollars on hand. The brakes had gone out on our car while we were in Tulsa and I had used much of our cash to pay for new ones, but now we found ourselves in a tricky situation.

"Don't worry," I told Mary Jo as I confidently drove toward St. Louis. "Our bank gave us an ATM card that is compatible with machines all over the world. We'll find an ATM machine in the next city."

This was in the early 1980s before ATM machines were common, but we pulled into the next city and began looking for a bank where we could withdraw money. I felt sure the trip would continue to go smoothly, but the first bank machine I went to refused my card.

"Sorry," it said, "your card is not compatible with our system."

We found another bank, but their machine would not accept my card.

"Sorry," it said, "your card is not authorized for withdrawals at this machine."

I walked back to the car and, like a balloon with a slow leak, our atmosphere of joy began to deflate.

"Daddy, I'm hungry," one of the kids said, while the other one fussed and squirmed.

"Daddy will find us a place to eat and sleep," I told them, and Mary Jo glanced at me to see if I believed my own words.

We had to get on the highway and drive further because none of the banks in that city would serve us, and then I had to fill the car up with gas which ate up the rest of the eighteen dollars. Suddenly we were hundreds of miles from home with not a cent to our names, night falling, stomachs growling, tempers rising and no prospect of relief. I began to grumble about our bank. Mary Jo sat silent, staring out the window and the kids began to cry.

"We're tired, Daddy!"

Our vacation had been so wonderful, and I wanted so much to stop at every hotel I saw going by, but we had no choice but to press on and find a bank machine that would help us.

City ... after city ... machine ... after machine. I stumbled blurry-eyed to each one only to have it tell me that my card was not authorized. In every new city I would pull the car off and look for a bank, then walk back to the car having failed again. I could barely stay awake and I knew everyone else was miserable.

By three o'clock in the morning we reached Kalamazoo, having driven through Oklahoma, Missouri, Illinois and Michigan, and I finally found an ATM machine that worked. In a daze I got money out and we found a hotel, though the beds were not nearly as comfortable as they would have been had we dived into them six hours earlier.

What began as a great drive home from a terrific vacation turned into a nightmare and a memory we can only laugh about many years later.

Our Christian life can be like that. We keep going down the road, stopping at one place after another looking for rest— a Bible study, a conference, a special service —but nothing seems to work for us anymore. We have lost our spiritual momentum.

What causes this weariness? Why do some crash? Why do some experience a dullness of spirit? Why do some get tired of God, tired of people and the journey goes sour? Why is it that the things that once excited us now seem stale? We go through the motions, but we do not have the passion anymore.

I have thought a lot about this, and believe there are clear causes for losing our momentum. As a backdrop to this I want to briefly look at the example of Elijah, who went through terrible burn-out.

The Discouraged Prophet

The great prophet Elijah was a man like you and me, with the same desires, passions and feelings that you and I have, and yet there was a time when he lost his momentum.

In First Kings 18, we read that a great contest had taken place between the true God and the god of Baal. Four hundred and fifty false prophets were slain by Elijah in one of the greatest displays of God's power in the entire Bible. Fire had fallen from Heaven and licked up the water they had used to douse the altar. There was Elijah, one man standing against a multitude, and he did not just win, he blew away the competition. Of course we know that God did it. Elijah was just a man, but he was a man at the pinnacle of achievement. I believe he thought the outcome of the contest would bring great revival to Israel.

How shocked he must have been when it did not.

King Ahab told his wife, Jezebel, what had happened.

> So Jezebel sent a messenger to Elijah to say, "May the gods deal with me, be it ever so severely, if by this time tomorrow I do not make your life like that of one of them."
>
> —1 Kings 19:2

Elijah wanted Jezebel and Israel to have a change of heart, to turn from false gods, to welcome the prophets of the true God, but Jezebel did exactly the opposite: She threatened to kill him, causing Elijah to run for his life.

> Elijah was afraid and ran for his life. When he came to Beersheba in Judah, he left his servant there, while he himself went a day's journey into the desert. He came to a broom tree, sat down under it and prayed that he might die...
>
> —1 Kings 19:3, 4a

This is what happens when we lose our motivation. We do not care if we live or die. We know we are going to Heaven, and we want to get there as soon as possible. We feel washed up, useless on this earth. That is how Elijah felt.

> "I have had enough, LORD," he said. "Take my life; I am no better than my ancestors..."
>
> —1 Kings 19:4b

It is not a sin to be down in the dumps once in a while, but there is nothing godly or righteous about *staying* down in the dumps. When we lose our motivation, we often feel like crawling into a cave, and that is exactly what Elijah did.

> **Then he went to a cave and spent the night. And the word of the Lord came to him: "What are you doing here, Elijah?" He replied, "I have been very zealous for the LORD God Almighty. The Israelites have rejected your covenant, broken down your altars, and put your prophets to death with the sword. I am the only one left, and now they are trying to kill me too."**
>
> **—1 Kings 19:9, 10**

Elijah then wrapped his face in his coat, stood in the cave's entrance, and the Lord came along again. When He asked Elijah what he was doing there, Elijah — depressed, discouraged and demotivated — answered with exactly the same words as before.

He was stuck. Burned out. Demotivated.

I was reading an article about how baby boomers are three hundred percent more depressed and discouraged than the previous generation. I believe it is because we have striven for success in the natural energies of our flesh and we have become demotivated.

Motivation is that inner miracle that causes us to be stimulated and excited, driving in a positive direction. Motivation is not accidental, any more than success and happiness are accidental. You will never see an accidentally successful person, or an accidentally motivated person.

God has given every man and woman motivation to achieve great things. Our part is to stir up that motivation — to motivate ourselves toward the goal God sets before us. That is faith action.

What happens when we lose our motivation?

First, we experience doubt and confusion. Elijah began to wonder if it was time for him to die. I have found that the devil often tries to steal our motivation right after a great success, like the success I had on the missions crusades in Africa. Elijah was the most successful prophet up to his time. He had raised a little boy from the dead, multiplied oil and flour for a widow, and called fire down from Heaven. Yet, he began to doubt God's Word and believe that Jezebel's power to kill him was stronger than God's power to keep him.

Jesus would later say to a certain group of people that they erred in two ways: Not knowing or believing the Scriptures, and not knowing the power of God. Elijah faltered in both. He was confused, tired, and full of doubt in those moments.

Secondly, when we lose our motivation, we procrastinate. Elijah slept under a Juniper tree, a symbol of self-pity, then crawled into a cave. He was called to bring revival to the nation of Israel, but he put it off. He did not want to take anymore risks: "I am not going to prophesy anymore, I am not going to work anymore miracles, I am not going to challenge the false religions anymore, because after everything I do for them, they want to kill me."

He put off the call on his life.

Thirdly, we lean on status symbols and titles rather than on faith in Jesus Christ. When we have lost our motivation we rely on props to keep us up. Elijah said, "I am a prophet, I am the only one." He started relying on his title rather than faith in God.

It is easy for us to do the same. We lean on our job title, or our accomplishments, or how much we gave to missions, or the nice compliment someone paid to us. Or we become fetish fiends, using cell phones and Mont Blanc pens to show people how important we are, but it is all a cover. When we find ourselves losing motivation we lean more on our titles and status symbols than we do on faith in Christ.

Fourth, complacency sets in. We become satisfied with mediocrity. We give into the spirit of "good enough."

Finally, we seem to lose our purpose and mission in life.

How do we grow weary? In the next chapter, we'll look at the major causes for losing momentum.

Chapter Four

Why We Lose Momentum

What causes the loss of momentum that Elijah suffered, and that many of us suffer?

Number One: Weariness at the wheel.

After a few thousand miles on the road, our original excitement begins to erode. When I was a boy my dad had a new Buick, the biggest car I had ever seen, and I used to wait for him to get off work and I would run to the end of the road to meet him. He would put me on his lap and let me steer the car all the way home. That was exciting at first, but soon the novelty wore off and I wanted to be in complete control. I wanted to push the gas pedal, too.

When I was twelve years old I thought I knew how to drive. I knew that "R" meant "Reverse," and "D" meant "go forward." One Saturday morning, while everybody was still in bed, I got the car keys, started the car up in the garage and put it in "R." Getting the car out of the garage was no problem, so I got braver. I hit the gas, still in reverse gear, and swerved into the house. There was a crashing sound, and I looked back and saw the damage I had done. For a brief moment I considered jumping out of the car and telling my parents I had caught someone trying to steal the car, but honesty got the best of me, and as I remember, my mom and dad "rearranged my parts" that morning.

There is excitement when you first learn to drive. A sixteen-year-old will drive anytime his parents let him, even to boring places like the grocery store. But later in life, like when you have to drive from Tulsa to Kalamazoo in one day, that excitement wears off. Weariness at the wheel comes from the journey and the daily erosion of our faith. It has caused many to lose control, to go off the road, to take the wrong exit. It causes us to lose our perspective, and we find ourselves talking about our feelings instead of the facts. We become self-critical, our mind seeks out every error we have made. We lose our sense of God's grace. It happened to Elijah, and it can happen to us.

Number Two: Running out of gas.

How long can you go on an empty tank? Some like to drive with the needle on "E," as if daring their car to finally stall. Those are the kinds of people you see walking on the side of the road with a red gas can. Life passes them by as they pay for their mistake.

> My strength is dried up like a potsherd.
>
> —Psalm 22:15a

A potsherd was a piece of clay that was once wet and pliable, but was baked in the sun and became brittle and worthless. Usually the hardest workers and the most dedicated people experience this when they try to work for God in their own energy. They run out of gas. As a pastor I see it often, and have learned that spending time with crowds of people will eventually harden your heart unless you spend as much time alone in the presence of God, which softens your heart.

Number Three: Disillusionment.

> All the counsel you have received has only worn you out!
>
> —Isaiah 47:13a

I know a man who was a powerful healing evangelists in the 1950s. He told me he became so disillusioned with the lack of integrity in finances, and the way some evangelists kept "sucker lists" of people they knew they could get money from, that he left the ministry. He was disappointed, discouraged, disillusioned and distracted. Those things are from the devil, not from God.

Number Four: Covetousness.

When David grew weary, he started isolating himself, and that led to unhealthy thoughts. He started drawing away from God, and he went from contentment to covetousness.

Contentment is being totally satisfied in the will of God; covetousness is when you have an inordinate desire for gain. It does not matter if that desire for gain is for something that seems spiritual. Some people actually covet God's anointing, or spiritual gifts, or a big ministry, not so that people will be healed, helped, blessed and lifted, but so people will think highly of them.

Paul told Timothy, "godliness with contentment is great gain" (1 Timothy 6:6). Jesus said:

> But seek first his kingdom and his righteousness, and all these things will be given to you as well.
>
> —Matthew 6:33

Then the devil says, "Brother so-and so has a speed boat, and you don't even have a rowboat." "Look at the anointing so-and-so has! And you have nothing." We start coveting a speed boat or someone else's spiritual gifts, and it brings weariness to our life; we grow faint. We find ourselves slowing down on this adventurous Christian road.

Years ago, when we went into a building program, my wife and I vowed to God that we would not move our personal residence until the house of the Lord was built. We read in Haggai how the people of God had neglected the house of God and put their personal comforts first. We were living in what had been my house as a bachelor, a two bedroom home with an old musty basement for my office. Every time I went down there to study I would have an allergic reaction to the mold.

Then the neighborhood started going downhill. Our neighbors had break-ins, and someone kicked in the next door basement window, threw a torch in and caught the house on fire. At a later time when we were trying to sell our house, a man pulled up and showed interest. He asked how we liked the neighborhood, and we said we never had any trouble. Just then a fight broke out across the street, and the neighborhood drunk came walking down the road yelling, "Mary Jo, I want a cup of coffee." That potential buyer drove off and we never saw him again.

It was getting discouraging. I had been there fourteen years and now we had two kids, a boy and a girl, and had to divide one tiny bedroom between them.

Then I went on a trip to preach overseas, and stayed with missionaries. Their home was twice as nice as mine: a lovely living room, dining room, bedroom and master bath. It seemed like a mansion compared to what I had.

On the way back I was discouraged about my own home, and I found myself going into a time where I lost my motivation, and I did not realize it was happening. I felt like God had let me down by making us live in a crummy neighborhood. I began to care less and less about the ministry, and was less grateful for what God had given me.

What a horrible time! My slide into demotivation began with the sinful habit of comparing myself to others, or to what I thought God owed me.

How did I get motivated again? I saw what was happening, recognized it as unthankfulness and turned it around. I thanked God for giving me good lungs, eyes, ears, legs and arms. I thanked Him that I live in such a prosperous society with so many comforts. I thanked Him for such a terrific church, a great wife and kids. Soon I could hardly hold my gratitude inside, and that house began to feel like a castle. We eventually moved into a bigger place in a nicer neighborhood, but my heart had already changed and I had regained my motivation.

Number Five: Failing to maintain your gift.

Imagine that you give your daughter a beautiful new car. One of the main things you would drum into her is the need to maintain it, get the oil changed, and get it tuned up once in a while. The same is true of the life that God gives us. I always wondered what Philippians 2:12 meant when it said, "continue to work out your salvation with fear and trembling." Now I believe it means that when God gives us a wonderful gift of eternal, abundant life, we are to take care of it! We maintain it, refuel it, repair it when necessary, and most of all, we use it. We do not let it sit in the garage.

In maintaining our spiritual life, we have to have regular check-ups. That is why Paul said to examine ourselves to see whether we are in the faith (2 Corinthians 13:5).

I forced myself to earn a master's degree because I wanted to stay mentally sharp and grow in knowledge. One of the courses I had to take was on planting churches for the next century, and I was not looking forward to it. Once I started reading the books though, I discovered that I was enjoying them. By the end of the course I was so excited that I called all of the pastors of our daughter churches and scheduled a meeting with them so I could pass on what I had learned. My vision more than doubled by doing that course. It was like a check-up for me. My vision had been too small.

We all need a check-up once in a while. We need to go to a conference, go to an extra prayer meeting, a seminar, or take a course. Maintain and upgrade your walk with Christ.

■ *Number Six: Putting the wrong products in the wrong place.*

When I was fifteen years old I worked at Jack Harner's Pure Oil gas station. He did not know I was fifteen and I did not bother telling him. I enjoyed making a dollar an hour. One day a guy pulled in and asked me to check his oil, and I pulled out the transmission dip stick and said it's a little low. I got a quart of 10W30 engine oil and put it in his transmission. After the boss caught me, it was too late.

You do not put engine oil in the transmission, or water in the gas tank, or gas in the radiator. We somehow got a little bit of water in our gas tank one time and the car sputtered, sparked and stalled for a week. We had to change the spark plugs and flush the engine out. Putting the wrong product in the wrong place costs a lot to repair.

Some people listen to negative teaching and it begins to dominate their views. Whether it is radio or television programs, books or web sites, there are some so-called ministers of the Gospel who feed fear. One woman from my church said she listened to a prophecy program three days in a row and went away feeling hopeless. If something makes you feel hopeless, you are putting the wrong thing in the wrong place. The Gospel is a Gospel of hope! If what you hear leaves you hollow, it is not God.

Proverbs says not to listen to teaching that contradicts the truth, because little by little it will pollute your mind.

Jesus came that we might have life more abundantly, not fear and negativity. He did not come to rip off your joy or steal your peace, but to restore them in full.

I know a man who once was a pastor but is out of the ministry today and has a bad drinking problem. I tried to counsel him at the beginning of his downfall when he started watching city council meetings and getting angry at every decision they made. I could see him getting more and more negative. That pastor went off at the wrong exit, and now is not helping anybody.

Number Seven: Continuing to drive while damaged.

When we drive, our car can sustain damage, which allegorically speaking I compare to Christians bumping and bruising each other on their way to the promised land. Being offended by what someone else says or does (or doesn't do) is like getting a nail in our tire. Ideally, when that happens we pull off, fix or replace the tire and get back on the road. We resolve the problem first, then go on.

But many people are offended and continue to drive at the same speed with a flat tire. The longer they go, the worse the damage gets.

The devil causes them to focus on a hurt or disappointment, and they continue to go forward with a nail sticking out of their tire. The right thing to do is not let that small injury turn into a bigger problem. If you feel offended, resolve it quickly as the Bible admonishes us to do. If you do not, it will eventually cause you to leave the Body of Christ.

A man once said to me that he firmly believed that God had added him to our church. A few weeks later he told me he was leaving the church because the music was too loud. Another lady told me she was offended because there were not Christian symbols hanging around the sanctuary and foyer. She left, too.

I had a musician tell me one time he was leaving the church because the guy in the sound booth was supposedly giving him dirty looks.

I have received letters from people who enumerated offenses that dated back an entire decade or more. But I have never seen anybody who nursed a hurt, rehearsed a grudge, or refused to forgive a past offense grow any further than where they were when they sustained their last offense. They seem to stall or go in slow motion.

One time I called a lady whose name I found in a church address book, and who had been a member of our church many years before. When I got her on the phone she told me, "I will never come to that church again. Back in 1964 the music minister said something mean to me." I said, "I'm sorry. We have a different music minister now." She said, "I do not care, I am never coming back. In fact I am never going to any church. I was offended, and besides I am crippled with arthritis."

Grudges are not only bad for the soul, but for the body as well. I have seen people healed of arthritis when they let go of an offense. Years ago a Catholic priest began to preach on the subject of forgiveness and he noticed something happened in his parish. People started being miraculously healed of maladies and conditions. He came to realize that forgiveness is a major key to spiritual *and* physical wellness.

John Bevere in his book *The Bait of Satan* says a person's future is determined by how they handle offenses. In Matthew 24:10 (KJV), Jesus said:

> **And then shall many be offended, and shall betray one another, and shall hate one an other.**

The devil says we owe it to ourselves to make things right, but from God's perspective that is like driving full speed with a flat tire.

I read a true story in Kate McVeigh's book *Get Over It*. She was in a church service and the pastor asked how many ministers were present. All the ministers stood up, but there was a lady minister sitting behind Kate in a wheelchair, and she could not stand so she raised her hand. The pastor went around and recognized each minister and completely passed over the little lady in the wheelchair who was waving her hand. Kate wondered if the woman took offense. Then, about forty-five minutes into the service, the pastor walked back to the lady in the wheelchair and said "Sister, God is showing me that a miracle is in store for you. Rise and be healed in the name of Jesus." That lady got up out of her wheelchair and started walking, then running. She had not walked in five years. When she came back to her seat, Kate turned around and said, "I have got to ask if you were offended when that preacher overlooked you the first time." The lady said, "The devil tempted me to be, but I realized that if I held a grudge in my heart I might miss a miracle, so I said no, I am not going to be offended."

That woman had love in her heart. The Bible says love that never fails; it does not mind being overlooked. Love does not have to be recognized. She quickly got the nail out of her tire and kept driving.

Jesus said offenses are going to come. We are all going to get hurt by other people, often accidentally. We need to quickly fix the hurt in our heart, and then move on.

What if David had become offended at his brother's snide remarks just before he slew Goliath? He probably would not have slain the giant.

What if Moses remained offended by Pharaoh's insults?

What if Joseph remained offended by his brothers' horrible treatment of him?

These men of God knew how to fix the flat and forget about it!

Even worse is when we take other people's offenses as our own. I read about a woman who had a flat tire on the highway. Somebody in a van pulled over to help her, and a truck came along and hit the van, killing three people. The point is not that we should ignore people who need help, but that there is danger in taking someone's hurt as our own. We should help offended people, but not let that help extend to ungodly agreement with their offense.

The solution for leaving offenses behind is found in Mark 11:25 where Jesus said:

> **And when you stand praying, if you hold any-thing against anyone, forgive him, so that your Father in heaven may forgive you your sins.**

We choose to forgive, or we are tormented and put into a prison whose bars are made out of our own grudges.

Number Eight: Spending extended time thinking about your personal failures.

The disciples must have felt horrible after Jesus died, knowing they deserted Him. But if they had stayed that way, the Gospel would not have gone around the world as it did. They had to forgive them-selves.

After thirty years of being a Christian, Paul said, "I still have not attained. In fact, I have made a lot of mistakes, and sometimes I feel like the worst apostle there is." But he continued, "I have fought a good fight, I have run the race, I have finished my course and now I am ready to go to Heaven." (See Philippians chapter 3.) He faced the same temptation to lose spiritual momentum, but kept on going.

No matter what you are feeling, keep your hand to the plow.

Before I became a pastor, Mary Jo and I had a fight one Sunday. I was the Sunday night song leader at the church. After our blowup I did not *feel* like coming in and leading the song service. I *felt* like calling the pastor and saying, "(Cough) Hello Pastor, (cough) I won't be there tonight. I caught a little something here." But I had already preached on divine healing and health, so he would have told me to take my own medicine!

The Bible says that an honorable man "keeps his oath even when it hurts" (Psalm 15:4). I *felt* like the worst Christian in the world because I knew nobody else fought with his wife, but I went to the pulpit and acted like I was feeling great, welcoming everybody, telling them how good it was to be in church that evening. All the while the devil was saying to me, "You are a failure." I was so distracted that while we were singing "Jesus Saves," I accidentally sang, "Jesus shaves, Jesus shaves."

But in the midst of that, and other mistakes I made that evening, God spoke to me and said, "David, you are not a failure." I stood there in the pulpit and said silently, "What?" He said, "You have had a failure, but that does not make *you* a failure. You did not treat your wife right this afternoon, but you are still more than a winner through Christ Jesus, even if you fail a thousand times."

I learned something that evening: You are only a failure when you give up and get off the road. When you stay on that road, no matter how many failures you have, you will not fail in God's eyes.

Number Nine: Putting our focus on the problems instead of the goal.

Elijah saw the problems without seeing a solution. In the Gospels, when Peter stepped out of the boat to walk on water, he only got into trouble when he paid more attention to the wind than to Jesus.

Number Ten: Believing the words of our critics instead of the word of God.

Elijah hoped that Jezebel would be saved, and when she was not, he was crushed in spirit.

No matter how hard you or I try to make things right, there will always be someone who criticizes. There will never be a time when one hundred percent of the people will admire or appreciate you. Jesus told His disciples:

> Woe unto you, when all men speak well of you!
>
> —Luke 6:26a (KJV)

Criticism brought Elijah down for a season. What did it do to Jesus? People called Him a drunkard and a glutton. One group of religious people said He was demon possessed. Did He say, *You mean I ate too much? Am I really a glutton? My whole ministry is going to be ruined. Maybe I am not the Messiah.* No, Jesus knew who He was.

Do you know who you are? You are the righteousness of God in Christ, more than a conqueror through Jesus Christ who loves you. You are the apple of His eye. Let His voice ring loud in your ears, and may the threats of your critics amount to nothing.

Watch The Dashboard!

Those are the causes of losing motivation. What are the warning lights on our spiritual dashboard that tell us it is happening? Here is a quick checklist. Which ones apply to you?

• *Warning Light Number One:* Busyness consumes your life.

• *Warning Light Number Two:* Your original excitement has eroded.

•Warning Light Number Three: Weariness has set in. You feel you are running in circles.

•Warning Light Number Four: Sloppiness and undependability have slipped in. You start missing commitments and appointments.

•Warning Light Number Five: You are irritated by small things.

•Warning Light Number Six: You feel trapped and want to run from your life.

•Warning Light Number Seven: You suspect that you have some illness or are dying prematurely.

•Warning Light Number Eight: A bitterness of spirit has a hold of you.

•Warning Light Number Nine: You are confronted with a crisis or temptation and feel too weak to withstand it.

•Warning Light Number Ten: You have quit the race.

If any of those apply to you, then you need re-motivation. In the next chapter we will look at how to get back on the Road to Success.

Chapter Five

Gaining Momentum Back

In San Diego there is a naval shipyard that houses decommissioned ships. These massive, sea-going hulks are dry-docked, stripped of everything of value and left to sit until someone finds a use for them.

One of three things happens to those ships.

• Number One: **They may be used as target practice for new rockets and missiles, until they finally sink.**

• Number Two: **They may be sold for scrap metal.**

• Number Three: **They may be re-conditioned and re-commissioned.**

A person who has lost his spiritual motivation has those same three options. The devil will use the person as target practice until he or she is finally sunk. Or the person becomes a vessel of dishonor, is cut up and put to less noble uses in the scrap yard. Or the person is re-conditioned and re-commissioned.

Anyone who has lost his spiritual momentum can be re-conditioned and re-commissioned.

Have you lost your motivation? Found yourself in a cave of discouragement or under a Juniper tree of self pity? Has your life become hum-drum instead of an exciting adventure?

Here are critical steps to regaining your spiritual momentum.

Number One: Receive Jesus Christ as your Savior.

It cannot be said enough.

> ..."If anyone is thirsty, let him come to me and drink. Whoever believes in me, as the Scripture has said, streams of living water will flow from within him." By this he meant the Spirit, whom those who believed in him were later to receive...
>
> —John 7:37-39

Jesus gives us energy, power, strength, gasoline for our life engine. Many people believe in Jesus, but not as the Scriptures say. They believe He existed, but do not give Him their lives, and so they have no power. I asked one lady if she had ever received Christ and she said, "Yes, every Sunday." I said, "How?" She replied, "I take communion."

That is not receiving Christ the way the Scriptures say. The Scriptures say to turn from sin and put your faith in Jesus Christ and what He did on the cross, believing in your heart that God raised Him from the dead and you shall be saved and become a child of God. He will give you spiritual momentum.

Number Two: Receive the truth of God's Word.

There is no substitute for reading and absorbing the truth of the Bible. It is as critical to the Christian journey as oil is to an engine.

> That ye might walk worthy of the LORD unto all pleasing, being fruitful in every good work, and increasing in the knowledge of God;
>
> Strenghthened with all might, according to his glorious power, unto all patience and longsuffering with joyfulness.
>
> —Colossians 1:10-11 (KJV)

Number Three: Praise the Lord with reckless abandon.

> Sing aloud unto God our strength: make a joyful noise unto the God of Jacob.
>
> —Psalm 81:1 (KJV)
>
> The LORD *is* my strength and song, and is become my salvation.
>
> —Psalm 118:14 (KJV)

It is strange what they call an orthodox church nowadays. People think it means silent churches, stained-glass windows and a fancy cross between two candles. We think an orthodox service means singing a few hymns, hearing a liturgy and a brief homily, praying, singing softly and going home.

None of those things points to orthodox Christianity. Jesus was not crucified on a fancy cross between two candles, but on an old rugged cross between two thieves.

Orthodox Christianity, as described in the book of Acts, was anything but quiet. When the apostles went into public, lame men walked, leapt and praised God aloud. Their meetings were interrupted by shaking buildings and loud, wind-like sounds as the Spirit blew through. They cast out devils, drew crowds, and even had frequent angelic visitations. They prayed, praised, and magnified God in full voice.

That is orthodox Christianity! If we are to maintain momentum, we need to join in praising God, without a thought for our reputation or dignity. David's wife accused him of demeaning the office of the king by dancing before the Ark of the Covenant, and David responded:

> **I will become even more undignified than this, and I will be humiliated in my own eyes.**
>
> **—2 Samuel 6:22a**

He knew the power of praising with abandon.

Number Four: Speak words of strength.

I learned long ago that you can tell the condition of a car by the sound it makes. The same is true of people. You can know their condition by their sounds. What do they say? Are they always rattling on about this or that? Does a stream of complaints issue from their mouths? Are they always knocking and pinging, showing signs of engine wear?

> Let the weakling say, 'I am strong!'
>
> —Joel 3:10b

When you feel weak, *say* you are strong because the Word of God tells you that you are. When you face a temptation say, "I am strong in the Lord Jesus Christ." Say with your mouth the things the Bible tells you are true, not the things you feel to be true. Feelings lie all the time, so why listen to them?

> Thou shalt also decree a thing, and it shall be established unto thee:
>
> —Job 22:28a (KJV)

You and I decree things in our lives with words.

Number Five: Make passivity your enemy.

Passivity means waiting for things to happen rather than making them happen. James 2:17 says that faith without action is dead. Having all the faith in the world will not do you any good until you put action to it. I have had people tell me, "Pastor, I am going to take a break for about a year. I have been working hard as an usher and in the choir. I need some time to refresh." Almost all of them are being used as target practice by the devil today. Passivity leads to disrepair.

Number Six: Ask God to clean the windshield of your vision.

Say, "God, show me the road I am to travel." When He does, the renewed vision will elevate you.

> 'Call to me and I will answer you and tell you great and unsearchable things you do not know.'
>
> —Jeremiah 33:3

Number Seven: Develop relationships with fuelers not drainers.

A drainer is like Judas Iscariot; he drains your energy, whines, criticizes, does not contribute. Drainers move slowly and have hidden agendas. They infect a group and hang onto the Body of Christ like a tick until confronted, and then they are hurt or offended when they leave.

A fueler is like Paul or Barnabas. They ignite your energy, encourage you on in the Lord, and refresh your soul.

I do not mean we should cut off relationships with drainers. They still need ministry, and can become fuelers, but our close relationships should be with fuelers.

Churches should be full of fuelers, and we should stick close to the Body when we have lost our momentum. There we can stop and rest, regroup and get back on the road. Church is where you refuel, absorbing an anointed atmosphere, hearing a message that teaches or guides you. We cannot just get refueled in private prayer and watching television evangelists.

A car engine is good, but all alone it will not take us anywhere. In the same way, Jesus has set up the Church to be His Body extended throughout the earth. He is the head, the most important part, but we are the body. In car terms, the church is made up of car seats, tires, transmission boxes, carburetors, power windows, antennas, trunks and glove compartments. With all the parts in place we can move forward together. God intended the Church to be a place of inspiration and rejuvenation, where we refuel each other's energy.

Number Eight: Go looking for a special awareness of the presence of God.

Elijah went looking for God's presence, but it was not in the fire, the earthquake, nor the wind. It was not in the sensational, but in the soft and quiet.

Many times when we lose our motivation we seek the sensational to revive us. We want glory bumps, but those go away and we find ourselves still demotivated.

Motivation is not always sensational. It can be the still small voice that God used to speak to Elijah.

Number Nine: Understand the law of change.

One of the biggest problems churches have is being threatened by change.

Change is the world's one constant. You are not the same person you were thirty minutes ago. Certain cells in your body have died and new cells have been born. Someone said you cannot step into the same river twice. It's always changing.

I get a kick out of people who say they want to be baptized in the Jordan River, the same river Jesus was baptized in. Yes, Jesus was baptized in the Jordan River, but it is not the same river today. That water is not the same water.

Unless we develop flexibility, we will lose our motivation when things begin to change. I think it is absolutely marvelous the way God moves in different and fresh ways. I have seen the faith movement, the Word movement, the church growth movement, the Jesus movement, the charismatic movement of the '70s and the revival movement of today, and I feel like I have been a part of it all. Why? Because I stay resilient and flexible.

Number Ten: Do not try too hard.

For the first five or six years of my ministry I tried so hard to please God and people and to do everything perfectly. I found out that when I do not try so hard, I do better than when I *do* try hard with my natural energies.

We can fizzle out trying to be perfect Christians. We fall short and get discouraged. God has an easy yoke for us, one that requires much work, but which fits us well and does not burn us out.

Instead of being intimidated by others, be inspired by others. I used to feel like an inferior minister, because every Sunday morning before church I would get up and pray and read the Bible, and at eight o'clock I would turn on the television and watch Rex Humbard's worldwide outreach ministry. I would see thousands of people in church, and I felt like a bum compared to him. I bought Rex's albums, and practiced his sermons in the mirror, but I thought there was no hope for another minister because Rex and others had all of the stations tied up.

Little did I know that ten years later that man I had admired every Sunday morning would kneel in my office and pray for God's anointing on my life and ministry. Little by little our church has grown, and now we are reaching more people today than Rex Humbard was when I was watching him on television. God did something. Today I am not intimidated or depressed by other people's ministries. I am much more comfortable with myself as a unique creation with unique talents that are not in competition with anybody else's. And I have learned not to try so hard but to let it flow naturally.

Number Eleven: Understand the law of strength.

Isaiah 40:31 is the secret of successful living.

> But they that wait upon the LORD shall renew *their* strength; they shall mount up with wings as eagles; they shall run, and not be weary; *and* they shall walk, and not faint.
>
> —Isaiah 40:31 (KJV)

As we wait on God, His strength imbues us with power.

Number Twelve: Take a vacation.

How many times have you been too tired, too demotivated to take even one step in a positive direction? It is time to get away from the televisions, radios, faxes, cell phones and e-mail and go somewhere to be inspired. Don't wait until the flame of your motivation has become a flicker, and then a burning ember, and finally cold ash.

If you are like me, you think about the money it takes to get away. I had to get over that. Vacations are not luxuries but necessities, and until you realize that you will suffer with demotivation. Now is the time to go into the wilderness, or up to the mountain, or out to the quiet sandy beach. Pick up a handful of sand and let it run through your fingers and say, "My God knows the number of grains of sand in my hand, and the number on this beach, and He knows me."

Number Thirteen: Evaluate your faith goals.

Have you forgotten your life goals? Even science will tell you, people with goals live longer, happier and healthier. The Christian life cannot be lived without faith goals.

Number Fourteen: Remember not only the Cross but the following Sunday.

Jesus went to the Cross for the joy set before Him. He knew there would be a resurrection day. As a result, millions and even billions have come into the family of God.

Now that you are re-motivated it is time to look at some of the more devious dangers along the Road to Success. When we are moving ahead at a good speed, the devil will try to lure us away from the destination. Read on and learn how to avoid his snares.

Chapter Six

Fatal Attractions

In case you have not heard, there is a rip-off artist loose in your neighborhood. He is stealing people's valuables, breaking into homes, killing where he can, and robbing old and young alike.

He does not like you, or your family. He knows you by name, your weaknesses, your strengths. He knows when you leave the house, and where you sleep.

His name is Satan, and he wants you dead.

You and I cannot change the way the devil feels about us. He hates us because we were created in the image and likeness of God, and he hates God. We are never going to change the devil's attitude toward us. He came to steal, kill and destroy. The Bible calls him the accuser, destroyer, devourer, thief.

Satan's goal, if he cannot kill us, is to rob us of real life. By real life I mean active, vigorous, fresh, strong, efficient, powerful and contagious living, the kind promised by the Bible.

John 10:10 is a verse that I call "the great divide," because it divides all of humanity into two categories and says that each of us is living on one side or the other. Here is what Jesus said:

> **The thief commeth not, but for to steal, and to kill, and to destroy: I am come that they might have life, and that they might have *it* more abundantly.**
>
> **—John 10:10 (KJV)**

Let me define "life" for you. The Greek word means to be possessed with vitality, to live actively and vigorously, to be extremely blessed, to be fresh and strong, efficient, powerful and contagious.

But Jesus did not stop there. He said life "more abundantly," which in the Greek means a rich existence, excessive, overflowing, a surplus, not merely enough to get by on but more than enough, profuse, extraordinary, superior, remarkable and magnificently excellent.

Can you imagine living like that? When somebody asks how you are doing, are you able to reply that you are having a rich existence, an excess of all kinds of blessings, an overflowing supply, a surplus, more than enough, doing profusely and extraordinarily superior and living in a masterfully excellent condition? That is what Jesus was saying.

You and I live on one side or the other of that verse. Either the devil is kicking us around and stealing our momentum, or we have the abundant life Jesus spoke about.

Billboards

The devil owns real estate along the Road to Success, and he puts up billboards to get us to take the wrong exits. Whenever I step into the pulpit on Sunday mornings I know there are people who have had a week of depression, loneliness, temptation, fights. There are probably a few that have contemplated suicide during the past week. Some feel like a dark blanket is covering the light of their life and they cannot seem to re-ignite the burner.

Others face enticements that become entrapments that bring enslavement. The devil has lured them off at the wrong exit, and they have a hard time finding their way back to the highway.

The devil does not have the authority in this earth to devour our life unless he can somehow usurp our authority, which is why he puts up those billboards.

Happiness this way!

Get off here and relax!

Indulge yourself! Take the next exit!

Jesus, when He died on the cross, beat the devil. Sin, sickness, disease and poverty should no longer be a part of a believer's life. But the devil puts up his advertisements, his enticements, his images that fascinate or magnetize us, and when we begin to fantasize getting off at the wrong exit, we are a breath away from leaving the Road to Success. That brings death. Loss of life. Destruction. A mess!

> When tempted, no one should say, "God is tempting me." For God cannot be tempted by evil, nor does he tempt anyone; but each one is tempted when, by his own evil desire, he is dragged away and enticed. Then, after desire has conceived, it gives birth to sin; and sin, when it is full grown, gives birth to death.
>
> —James 1:13-15

I have found that if the devil cannot get a Christian to go to hell, he will try to get him or her to Heaven faster, but he has to lay traps, and he has to have enticements in those traps.

Mouse Traps

A while back my cat died after nineteen years of love and affection, and we started noticing mouse droppings in the basement and under the sink. Papers were chewed by a little animal of some sort. We knew that there must be a mouse in the house. Mary Jo said, "Dave, I think we have got a mouse." I said, "We have never had a mouse." She said, "But we have always had a cat. Now that he is gone, the mouse sees his opportunity. Would you get some traps?"

I went down to the store and bought some mousetraps. I knew that to catch a mouse you put something appealing in the trap, so I read up on the subject and found that cheese with peanut butter on it will attract mice faster than cheese alone because the scent is stronger. I put peanut butter on a piece of cheese, set the mousetrap and put it under the sink.

We came home from church and Mary Jo said, "Dave, would you look under the sink? I am afraid to open the door." I opened it and there was a little mouse pinned flat to the trap with his eyeballs popping out. He was dead!

I had to entice that mouse with something that attracted him (or her). The devil has to entice us with something that is going to fascinate us or lure us into his trap. That enticement brought death to the mouse because he acted on his desire for that peanut butter and cheese. The devil will put an enticement in our path, something to lure us into thoughts about something that is contrary to God's will.

How It Happens

There are at least seven steps in the cycle of sin.

Number One: There is a hidden lust.

Number Two: An enticement comes along to draw out that lust.

Number Three: The lust comes to the surface.

Number Four: Is the conception of the sin.

The Bible says, "when sin hath conceived." That does not mean action — yet. Conception is a two-fold word that means you have more than a buried lust, but an active desire. You meditate on it; start making plans in your mind. At first you may reject it and recoil. But when lust has conceived, the mind lays the groundwork for the action.

Our wonderful imaginations are employed for awful ends when sin is conceived in our minds. It happened to David, a man after God's heart, a mighty warrior, anointed king, composer of beautiful psalms, a worshiper. Hidden lust bubbled to the surface when he saw a woman bathing and he began to conceptualize what he wanted to do, how he would get her in his bedroom.

He was able to choose his sin, but he could not choose the consequences of sin. Twenty seconds of ecstasy brought the sword of pain and torment to David's home for the rest of his life. His young son died. His daughter was raped. His other son was murdered, and his son Absalom tried to overthrow David and his kingdom, then was yanked off his horse by a low-hanging tree limb and was stabbed. Where did it begin? In David's heart all those years before.

Number Five: The birth of the sin, taking action on the lust that was conceived.

Number Six: The growth and strengthening of the sin.

Number Seven: Death.

Let me return to the first step: lust. Usually when we think about lust we think about sexual lust. But lust means more than that. It is any desire contrary to God's revealed best for you. The devil will say, "God is cheating you. There is another way to achieve happiness without all these rules. You can get around it." Many people want to be wealthy, but they do not want to do it God's way. They do not want to give in order to receive. They want to hoard. They do not want to love or forgive or be faithful to the Lord.

I meet so many people in terrible situations who say they do not know how it happened to them. One young man I met had purple blotches all over his face. He was raised in church and knew God, but was pulled away by an enticement. He was curious about the concept of homosexuality, and tried it thinking the desire would subside, but it grew bigger and sin gave birth to death. The day before he died, a pastor I know interviewed him. By this time the man had repented and given his life back to Christ, but his words still ring in my ears: "I never thought this would happen to me." It was all he could do to gasp for breath.

We can lust after material possessions and wealth. Do you think of your retirement plan more than you think about the Bible? Do you ponder the fate of your stock picks more than you do God's plan for your life? Riches and wealth are not bad, but lust for riches will choke the effectiveness of the Word of God in your life.

Balaam is the classic example. He was a prophet who gave some of the most beautiful messianic prophecies in the Bible. One day the Midianite king asked him to curse the children of Israel. At first Balaam recoiled, but when the king offered him riches, his mind began to change. He was enticed.

The Bible says if you bless God's people you will be blessed, if you curse God's people, the curse comes on you. You cannot curse what God has blessed, and Balaam knew that, but the growing pot of gold promised to him drew him in. He said he wanted to pray about it, and it is a reasonable guess that he was not praying but conceptualizing. He may have even been thinking of using the riches for good purposes, perhaps to justify his greed. Finally, he figured out a way to get the people of God cursed without having to do it himself. He told the Midianite king to send beautiful Midianite women among the Israeli men so they would start intermarrying, contrary to God's command. After a while, Balaam said, God would curse His own people.

The plan worked. The Hebrew men married the Midianite women, and the women led their husbands into devil worship. Soon God could no longer bless His people. He withheld His blessings, and curses came on God's people. What happened to Balaam? He became a famous soothsayer, an occult teacher proclaiming to be a prophet of God. And when Israel repented and wiped out the Midianites, Balaam was slaughtered right along with them.

The lust for riches led to death.

New Wisdom?

There is lust for pleasure, drunkenness, power and prestige. There is even a lust for wisdom, believe it or not. I have seen Christians lose out with God because they go after "new wisdom" contrary to the wisdom found in Jesus Christ. The Bible says that in Him are hidden all the treasures of wisdom and knowledge (Colossians 2:3). Some people grow tired of God's wisdom and start looking in other religions or philosophies. I knew a man of God who was brought down because he got into transcendental meditation. His teachers told him it was compatible with all religions, but he did not know that they were chanting to Hindu gods. Eventually, his life fell apart.

In World War II, an enemy island was taken by American soldiers. They went searching for hidden enemy soldiers, and in a cave they found cases of liquor. The men broke open the bottles and drank the liquor, and every one who did died because it was laced with poison. The enemy knew that the Americans would be enticed by free alcohol.

There is a lust for time. Some people are so enticed by it that they give up their spiritual life, allocating that time to other pursuits.

At its most basic level, lust is anything that puts our self-interest and desires first. How do we know if we are being pulled off the Road to Success and toward a fatal attraction? In the next chapter, we will see.

All confidence, when it comes to spiritual things, must be in Jesus Christ.

Chapter Seven

Red Flags On The Road To Failure

Thankfully, God has given us red flags on the Road to Failure that warn us if we are about to take a wrong exit. All of us have wept bitter tears over our mistakes. We have said things we wished we had not said, done things we wished we had not done.

God Of A Thousand Chances

I believe no mistake happens suddenly and without warning, but there are stages.

For six years I was on a board of leaders for my denomination, and one of our responsibilities was to handle cases of ministers who fell into sin. So many times I sat across the table from people who were dejected because they had failed in one way or another. They all said the same thing. "I do not know what came over me. I cannot believe it was me." They had not heeded the warning flags along the Road to Failure.

In the business world there is a saying, "He who stumbles on the same rock twice deserves to break his neck." Fortunately, Jesus never felt that way. If He did, Peter would have never made it, and neither would the rest of us. Peter seems impetuous in the Gospels, like he was making mistake after mistake, but in Mark 14:72 we find him weeping the bitter tears of defeat. He had probably made one of the most serious failures anyone could make — he denied the Lord. After all, Jesus said that if we confess Him before men, He will confess us before the Father, but if we deny Him before men, He will deny us before the Father.

And yet He is the God of another chance, even after we make a serious mistake and take the wrong road.

Perhaps no one has made a more well-known mistake than the apostle Peter. His experience shows us the red flags that warn us away from wrong exits and lusts of all kinds.

> While Peter was below in the courtyard, one of the servant girls of the high priest came by. When she saw Peter warming himself, she looked closely at him. "You also were with that

Nazarene, Jesus," she said. But he denied it. "I don't know or understand what you are talking about," he said, and went out into the entryway. When the servant girl saw him there, she said again to those standing around, "This fellow is one of them." Again he denied it. After a little while, those standing near said to Peter, "Surely you are one of them, for you are a Galilean." He began to call down curses on himself, and he swore to them, "I don't know this man you're talking about." Immediately the rooster crowed the second time. Then Peter remembered the word Jesus had spoken to him: "Before the rooster crows twice you will disown me three times." And he broke down and wept.

—Mark 14:66-72

Red Flag Number One: Self-confidence.

Well before this famous scene of betrayal, Peter's first flag was waving before his eyes, but he did not see it. Earlier that night, Jesus had told his disciples they would fall away in accordance with the Scripture that says:

...I will strike the shepherd, and the sheep will be scattered.

—Mark 14:27b

Peter declared, "Even if all fall away, I will not."

—Mark 14:29

Peter boasted in his self-confidence. He truly believed that by his own effort he could stay on the right road. Modern Christians fall into this trap more often than we think. How many times do we hear about another person's failure and recoil in shock saying, "I do not know how they could have done that!" If we respond that way to somebody else's failure, be warned: That is the first red flag on the road to our own failure.

Self-confidence is an admired trait. We all want people that are self-confident and self-assured in business, politics, sports and most types of leadership, but to transfer it to spiritual things is dangerous. Jesus said that without Him, we can do nothing.

> ...apart from me you can do nothing.
>
> —John 15:5

> Except the LORD build the house, they labor in vain that build it.
>
> —Psalm 127:1 (KJV)

> ...'Not by might nor by power, but by my Spirit,' says the Lord Almighty.
>
> —Zechariah 4:6b

All confidence, when it comes to spiritual things, must be in Jesus Christ. Paul said in Philippians 3:3 that he had *no* confidence in the flesh.

I remember a minister who became very successful and received many invitations to teach others how to be successful. He built a great church and seemed to have learned the formula for church growth. Then, unknown to anyone else, a woman came into his life and he was enticed by his own lusts. During the se-

cret affair he continued to be incredibly self-confident. He felt he no longer needed to pray because he
had it down to a methodology. In the end he found
himself in a cheap motel room, overridden by guilt.
He then commited suicide to the shock of everyone.
It started with putting confidence in self rather than
confidence in God.

We cannot believe our own press reports. The
scouts told General Custer that it would take three
to four days to wipe out the Sioux Indians and that
he had better call for back-up support. He replied,
"We will have this battle over in less than a day and
we do not need any support." Custer was right about
one thing: the battle lasted less than a day, but the
outcome was the opposite of what he thought it
would be.

Paul said in Romans:

> For by the grace given to me I say to every one
> of you: Do not think of yourself more highly than
> you ought, but rather think of your self with so-
> ber judgment, in accordance with the measure
> of faith God has given to you.
>
> —Romans 12:3

And in 1 Corinthians he said:

> So, if you think you are standing firm, be care-
> ful that you don't fall.
>
> —1 Corinthians 10:12

97

All our confidence and trust must be in Jesus Christ. He is the one who died on the cross and rose from the dead.

Red Flag Number Two: Disputing God's words.

"I tell you the truth," Jesus answered, "today — yes, tonight — before the rooster crows twice you yourself will disown me three times. But Peter insisted emphatically, "Even if I have to die with you, I will never disown you. "

Peter disputed the Word of the Lord. He thought he knew better. He honestly did not believe what Jesus said.

What a danger! If the Lord tells us something, whether we find it incredible or not, we had better believe it. He tells us things about ourselves not to hurt us, but to help us.

Red Flag Number Three: Lack of prayer.

The third red flag came up when Jesus went into the garden to pray and asked His friends to pray with Him, but instead of praying, they fell asleep. Jesus needed them more than ever in that moment.

Prayer is the secret ingredient to success. I have interviewed dozens of failed Christians, and have concluded one thing: Prayerlessness is the cause of all Christian failure. Every failure begins with prayer failure. It is like cavities that build up in the teeth after years of daily neglect. Missing a day of brushing here and there does not seem important until your dentist says you have a mouthful of rotting teeth.

Fortunately, prayer works powerfully against failure. We accomplish more with a few faith-filled prayers than with years of prayerless work. Prayer must be at the top of the priority list.

It was not too many years ago that a jet with a major airline was flying from New York to Miami, and when they put the landing gear down, the landing gear light did not come on. The pilots put the plane on autopilot, circling the Everglades while they thumped the light trying to get it to work. They could not land if they were not sure their landing gear was down.

But one of the pilots accidentally turned the autopilot off and the plane began to lose altitude. All the while the pilots were fooling around with a seventy-five-cent light bulb!

I have a pilot's license, and one of the things I learned was that priorities go in this order: aviate, navigate, communicate. Aviate means to keep the plane flying. Second priority is to navigate, get to where you are going. Third priority is to communicate. Never try to make radio contact if a plane is in a spin. The point is to have the most important things under control before moving on to the next important thing.

While those pilots were fooling around with a light bulb, the plane crashed into the Everglades and the passengers and pilots were killed. They lost sight of the fact that their first priority was to aviate. Prayer is the Christian's first priority.

Red Flag Number Four: Using carnal weapons.

In Mark 14:47 we are told that one of them that stood by Jesus when He was arrested drew a sword and smote the servant of the high priest, cutting off his ear. John tells us it was Peter.

The weapons of our warfare are not carnal, Paul said, but mighty through God to the pulling down of strongholds.

> **For the weapons of our warfare *are* not carnal, but mighty through God to the pulling down of strong holds.**
>
> **—2 Corinthians 10:4 (KJV)**

One of the ways Christians have bought into carnal warfare is in thinking that political or social influence equals spiritual power. Many pulpits in America have drowned out the message of Jesus Christ in favor of political messages. If Christians would forget the petitions and placards for a while and hold prayer meetings instead, we would accomplish more.

Of course there has to be a balance. I vote and am concerned about our nation. I advise politicians and govermental leaders when they call me for help. But we have to remember what the prize is. It is not control of Congress or the White House. It is the privilege of serving Jesus, lifting Him up and letting men and women be attracted to Him.

In the same way, if we try to fight our personal battles with human forces or wisdom, we are doomed to fail. God has a plan for each of the difficulties we face, but we must trust Him and not force a solution with carnal weapons.

Red Flag Number Five: Following Jesus afar off.

Mark 14:54 tells us Peter followed Jesus afar off, or at a distance. He did not want to get too close lest he endanger his own life.

We are not called to follow Jesus afar off but up close. I want to be where the miracles are — they are with Jesus!

You can always tell when somebody wants to follow Jesus afar off. They are the ones who pose questions with the intent of starting an argument. "Pastor Williams, is it allowable for a Christian to drink alcohol? Dance? Listen to secular music?" If you say no to those things, they pounce on you and talk about Christians throughout history who drank alcohol and turned secular songs into church hymns. They are more concerned with finding where the edges are than in pressing toward the center.

If we want to avoid failure, we must press in close, not lurk in the shadows.

Red Flag Number Six: Finding warmth at the enemy's fire.

Peter comforted himself by the enemy's fire. We do the same thing when we find security in an ungodly situation or habit. Whenever we find our security in this world, a red flag is waving.

Peter failed as we all do sometimes. He had six warning flags along the way — and probably a lot more than that — but he was restored. Now I want to compare Peter's reaction to Judas' reaction. Both men failed and took the wrong exit, but only one got back on the Road to Success. Both men had moments of great grief when the weight of their guilt fell upon them.

> ...Then Peter remembered the word Jesus had spoken to him ... And he broke down and wept.
>
> —Mark 14:72b

> When Judas, who had betrayed him, saw that Jesus was condemned, he was seized with remorse...
>
> —Matthew 27:3a

Somehow, Judas did not go beyond remorse and Peter did. Judas decided not to change, and he hanged himself. Peter had a sincere change of heart. He wept with sharp, violent sobs. He was broken. He did not blame anyone else, but he also did not disqualify himself from future ministry. He knew enough about grace to know that God could restore him. He found the on-ramp and steered back on to the Road to Success.

Peter's failure became an asset because it proved to him that he could do nothing of value in his own effort. He became much more useful to Jesus after learning this lesson, and it was Peter who preached the first sermon after the crucifixion and saw thousands saved. Peter flunked one test, but aced the next one. In fact, he flunked three times in a row, every time he denied he knew Jesus; but God does not mothball us that quickly. He recommissions us, sends us on new journeys into the Sea of Success — even after great failures.

How To Steer Clear Of Fatal Attractions

Here are three quick principles to help you avoid those fatal attractions the devil advertises to you.

•*Quick Principle Number One:* **Make purposeful choices to live right, think right and act right according to God's revealed plan.**

The Bible tells us that Daniel *purposed in his heart* not to eat the king's meat, but to live by God's dietary laws. He was wiser and more radiant than everyone else.

•*Quick Principle Number Two:* **Fill your life with God's Word.**

> I have hidden your word in my heart that I might not sin against you.
>
> —**Psalm 119:11**

> ..."If you hold to my teaching, you are really my disciples. Then you will know the truth, and the truth will set you free."
>
> —**John 8:31b**

When an enticement comes, the Word of God can rise up from within you and give the enticement the response it deserves. When the devil confronted Jesus, the Lord said, "It is written: 'Man does not live on bread alone, but on every word that comes from the mouth of God'" (Matthew 4:4). He spoke the Word and the devil left Him. When you speak the Word of God to an enticement, the enticement dies and you live. If you speak about the enticement and conceptualize it in your mind, *it* lives and *you* die.

• *Quick Principle Number Three:* Pray in advance.

Jesus taught us to pray. "And lead us not into temptation, but deliver us from the evil one" (Matthew 6:13). That means, "do not let us fall into the grip of enticing temptations." If we prayed more advance prayers, we would have to pray less emergency prayers.

Does God really care if we get off the Road to Success? Does He care if we are dragged away by our own lusts? Yes! In the next chapter we will look at one of the most misunderstood aspects of God's character to see why He cares.

There is nothing quite so heartbreaking as loving someone deeply, completely, and totally and not having that love returned to you.

Chapter Eight

The Broken Heart Of God

Sometimes we think of God as the Great Mr. Spock in the Sky, a Being with no emotions, no feelings, no heart strings, no way of feeling emotional pain. But the Bible says that God has feelings, that His heart can ache and hurt and grieve. And He does grieve when we get off the Road to Success.

In the sixth chapter of Ezekiel, God told the children of Israel the terrible things that would come upon them if they served other gods. Then He said something extraordinary:

> ...how I have been grieved by their adulterous hearts, which have turned away from me, and by their eyes, which have lusted after their idols.
>
> —Ezekiel 6:9b

God felt emotional pain because the eyes of His people were filled with spiritual adultery, their hearts with other passions.

There is nothing like the experience of loving somebody and having him or her love you in return. I know what it is like to have a wife and children who love me with genuine love.

But there is nothing quite so heartbreaking as loving someone deeply, completely, and totally and not having that love returned to you. That is the situation God was in. He poured out His love to Israel, brought them out of slavery, gave them a nation flowing with milk and honey, conquered their enemies for them, and they slapped Him in the face by serving other gods.

Sad to say, we all have done the same thing. One way or another we have rejected God, maybe years ago, maybe yesterday, maybe in a big way, maybe in a small way. We have left the Road to Success and sought other paths we thought would bring us greater pleasure, and in turn, God's heart broke over us.

Taking God For Granted

Does God's heart really break? Yes. He made man to love Him. He wanted somebody to pour His love into and somebody that would reciprocate that love.

He wanted you and me, our hearts, our devotion, just like a woman wants her groom's utmost devotion.

Recently I got a new computer and was learning how to use it. One day I turned it on and it said, "I love you, Dave." One of my staff had programmed it to surprise me with those words.

That computer can only spit out what someone puts into it, no matter how much we hear about artificial intelligence. It has no capacity to really love or to make personal choices. It's just a machine.

Choice is a key component of love. I could try to force somebody to love me, but it is not meaningful if it does not come from the heart. God chose Israel, but Israel chose the lifestyle of other nations, and as they adopted that lifestyle, they also adopted the false gods. Their love for God grew cold. Their religious rituals became empty.

God's response to all this was a broken heart. Imagine that your spouse comes home one night well after bed time claiming he or she had a flat tire. Imagine that it happens again and again until you realize he or she is seeing someone else. It would break your heart!

God felt the same way. When I was a youth pastor, I would watch as girls rejected offers from good looking, Bible-believing, Christ-loving guys, but threw themselves at dangerous, non-committed jerks who had no respect for women and bragged about their exploits. It always ended in disaster.

False gods are like bad boyfriends. They may seem daring or full of charm, but they are horrible lovers, and in it only for themselves. God grieves when we fall into the arms of another, not just because He is jealous for us, but because He knows the harm it will bring. No one embraces the devil without being scathed.

Other "gods"

What gods did the children of Israel choose instead? First was Molech, the god of pleasure and comfort. Apparently, God's blessings were not good enough for them, and they took for granted the prosperity He had given them. They wanted to direct their own pursuits so they made decisions based not on what the Lord said, but on their own desire for comfort, ease and entertainment. The New Testament says people will be "lovers of pleasure, more than lovers of God" (2 Timothy 3:4).

The second god they worshiped was Ashterah, the goddess of illicit sex. God had given the Israelites the marriage covenant, but they desired freedom from the constraints of marriage.

The third god they worshipped was Baal, the god of intellectualism and knowledge apart from the wisdom of almighty God.

The fourth god they worshipped was Mammon, the god of power and money. Many of the Israelites became workaholics so they could have more money or gain more power.

Each of these gods reminds me of the gods people worship in the modern world. They want instant pleasure more than long-term devotion, divorce rather than fidelity, man-centered wisdom rather than God's wisdom, and power and money more than anything else. We sometimes choose distractions, fatal attractions, enticing billboards and wrong exits before we choose God.

When we are in tune with the heart of God, we flee from failure because we do not want to hurt Him. We stay faithful to Him for the same reason we stay faithful to a spouse and children; because we care about how they feel.

Have you broken the heart of God? Do you feel the sting of hurting your Lover? He wants to restore you, and in the next chapter we will find out how God provides for us when we have failed.

When we have failed
God, we often need a place
of comfort, of rest,
of solitude.

Chapter Nine

Our Place Of Refuge

Think about your last vacation, driving down the highway for hour upon hour to reach the Grand Canyon, or Disneyland, or Grandma's house. After a while, everyone starts asking the inevitable question: "When are we going to stop?" Then there is a sign for a rest area. Fifty miles. Thirty-five miles. Twenty miles. Anticipation builds and passengers crane their necks to see the coming oasis. When Dad pulls over and parks next to the lush, green lawn complete with picnic tables and shade trees, everyone feels great relief. Kids run, Mom stretches her legs, Dad takes a jog and enjoys the scenery.

There is nothing more American than a rest area. A good one is like a safe harbor, a place of refreshment. All of us need times to relax.

When we have failed God, we often need a place of comfort, of rest, of solitude. God provides such places for us. In Old Testament times the nation of Israel had rest areas, though of a slightly more permanent variety. Joshua 20 talks about cities of refuge which were meant for anyone who had killed another person by accident. I am not sure how one person killed another by accident, or why cities were needed to protect such people, but when we dig a little deeper we find that God was revealing His character and nature through these cities of refuge.

The Lord told Joshua to assign six cities as cities of refuge. Their names are important:

> **So they set apart Kedesh in Galilee in the hill country of Naphtali, Shechem in the hill country of Ephraim, and Kiriath Arba (that is, Hebron) in the hill country of Judah. On the east side of the Jordan of Jericho they designated Bezer in the desert on the plateau in the tribe of Reuben, Ramoth in Gilead in the tribe of Gad, and Golan in Bashan in the tribe of Manasseh.**
>
> **—Joshua 20:7, 8**

Let me summarize the names:

- Kedesh

- Shechem

- Hebron

- Bezer

- Ramoth

- Golan

Why would they need six cities? Was God expecting a lot of accidental deaths? I don't think so. I believe God was using this to point to His Son, Jesus Christ.

You see, in Old Testament times, God gave covenant names so people would understand who He was. He was Jehovah-Tsidekenu, the one who gives righteousness, Jehovah-M'Keddesh, the one who sanctifies, Jehovah-Rophe the one who heals, Jehovah-Jireh, the prosperity giver, the provider, the promise-keeper, and Jehovah-Shalom, the peace giver. In the New Testament, all those attributes were embodied in one Person and one Name — Jesus. He became our refuge for any trouble.

We all want a place of safety and refuge. It sounds trite, but I remember a day when people did not have to lock their homes or cars because robbery was so infrequent. And we never worried about violent crimes. These days it is the fool who does not have a security system in his house, if he can afford it. One of the neighbors where I once lived had a sign in his window with a picture of a gun aimed right at you, and it read, "Don't even think about it!"

I read about a man who put a sign on his door whenever he ran errands that said, "Sally, do not come in, the boa constrictor is loose again."

People want security, protection, and a place where they can leave their worries on the doormat. God knew this, so he set up six cities of refuge.

Rest Area One: Our Road-Side Shower

The first place was Kedesh, meaning "holy place, a refuge for the unclean, the defiled, and the polluted." We know that sin pollutes and makes people unclean before God. But while we were sinners, Christ died for us. That old city of Kedesh is probably long gone, but the spirit of that city lives on in Jesus. He is our Kedesh, our place of refuge when we feel unclean or defiled. How many times in the New Testament do we see Jesus casting out unclean spirits? When the unclean came to Him, His touch made them clean. Kedesh is God's way of saying that when we realize we are hopelessly polluted without Him, He makes us clean and holy again.

Rest Area Two: Our Shoulder

The next city was in Shechem, meaning "shoulder" which indicates it was a refuge for the weary, vexed, exhausted, fatigued and burdened. Life gets tough at times, and the load seems too big. Many people feel they are caught in the spin cycle, with the energy being squeezed out of them by a tremendous centrifugal force. Every day has some new task or trial to wear us down.

Worn down people need a shoulder to lean on. Some need to be carried over the Shepherd's shoulders to rest for a while. Jesus said:

> **Come to me, all you who are weary and burdened, and I will give you rest.**
>
> **—Matthew 11:28**

Jesus is our Shechem. He will take our load if we give it to Him.

Rest Area Three: Our Fellowship

The third city was Hebron, which means "fellowship." It was a refuge for the homeless, forsaken, outcast, desolate and disposed of. There have been a number of international situations in recent years when we all saw refugees fleeing certain countries, their faces haunted by fear and anxiety, their eyes asking, "Where can I go where I will be safe?"

Jesus is the Hebron for the soul. Only He brings us fellowship and a home with our Heavenly Father. God is God over every person, whether he or she believes in Him or not. But He is only a Father, provider and home-giver to those who have come to Him through Jesus Christ.

Jesus said:

I am the way and the truth and the life. No one comes to the Father except through Me.

—John 14:6

We have fellowship with the Father through His Son. There are many forsaken and disposed people in the world. It makes me think of lepers in Jesus' day. Their odyssey began when they found a little white spot on their hand, went to the priest and were told, "It is leprosy. You must leave your home and go to a leper colony, or wander by yourself. If anybody comes within fifty feet of you, yell, 'Unclean, unclean!' so they do not get too close." Such a man could not even kiss his wife or children good-bye. He would never know the joy of seeing his children grow, or of holding his grandchildren.

But Jesus freely touched lepers and not only healed them but restored their fellowship with family and society. In a sense, that is what He does for each one of us, taking away our sin — much worse than leprosy — and restoring us to the family of God.

Rest Area Four: Our Public Defender

The fourth city was Bezer, a stronghold for the helpless, those with nobody to go to bat for them. Have you ever faced a situation where you felt no one was fighting for you? I read an article by a woman who was at a swim club where a mother was teaching a three-year-old girl to swim. The girl would not put her face in the water, and the mother was saying, "You are a little coward. Your dad is going to be so ashamed of you." The three-year-old began to cry, and there was nobody to go to bat for her.

Jesus is our Bezer, our advocate, the one who will go to bat for us and never lose.

A minister I know, a very Christ-like man, had a dream in which he died and stood before the gates of Heaven. "Sorry," the angel said. "Your name is not in the book." The minister said, "There must be some mistake." And they took him before a judge who asked one question after another.

"Did you live a righteous life?"

"Were you always kind and loving to other people?"

"Were you always honest and just in everything you did?"

To every one he had to honestly answer "no." Just when he felt that all hope was gone, the throne lit up and a voice more beautiful than a mother's voice filled the archways of the judgment seat. It said, "Father, even though this one had failures and faults in life, he professed to know Me. I took his place in judgment."

The minister woke up with an intense awareness of his need for grace, and he saw what it means to have a Savior who is our Bezer.

Rest Area Five: Our Hope

City number five was Ramoth, which means "exalted, a refuge for the hopeless, the despondent, the empty." Some people go through life with their stomach in knots, wondering, "Is life ever going to work out?" Hopelessness blankets their nights and they slow down on the road toward their God-given destiny.

But Jesus knows and can help us in that situation. He is the city of refuge called Ramoth, that beautiful rest area where we can pull in, put the seat back and relax. He is the hope-giver, the dream-inspirer, the void-filler. When we feel we can no longer go on, and when the future holds no brightness, there is a place for us.

Life was draining out of the little lady with the issue of blood in the Gospels. Twelve years of going to doctors, and only getting worse. But Jesus turned her hopelessness into hope — and healing.

The centurion, a father whose daughter was dying, sought refuge in Jesus. A hopeless situation turned into a miracle.

Rest Area Six: Our Escape

The final city was Golan, which means "a refuge for those tempted, seduced, allured, enticed, and on the edge of failure and defeat." We can run to Jesus because He gives us strength in the time of need. He was in all points tempted as we are, and is able to make a way of escape from sin.

The beautiful thing about it all is that we do not need to run to a particular geographic place to find our city of refuge. Whatever it is we need, we go to Jesus; our Kedesh, our Bezer, Ramoth, Hebron, Golan, Shechem — our city of refuge.

Snake eggs can be planted in your mind...and one day they will hatch.

Chapter Ten

Snake Eggs

One of the biggest distractions on the Road to Success is sexual temptation. Sex is a wonderful and beautiful gift from God — valuable, pleasurable, enjoyable, fun, exciting, adventurous. But there is an onslaught from hell that seeks to pervert and degrade it.

One time Mary Jo and I were at a hotel for a meeting of ministers in our denomination, and as she was getting ready in the bathroom I was fooling around with the television. I do not remember touching anything special on the remote, but as I flipped through the channels I came to one where a couple was having sex. It was graphic pornography. My heart began to beat fast and I wanted to turn that thing off as fast as I could; but another part of me wanted to see a little more. Mary Jo could hear the moans and groans the people were making on the television, so she stepped into the room and screamed, "Shut it off!" and I said, "I'm trying!" It was on for less than ten seconds.

That night I had to drive back to Lansing, and the whole time I felt filthy and perverse. I asked myself, "If Mary Jo had not been there, would I have followed the pull of my own desires or the pull from God?" I felt that somehow my anointing was hurt and all the way back I prayed: "God, forgive me. Get this image out of my mind." As anyone who has seen it knows, pornography leaves what feels like an indelible mark on the brain.

The Cockatrice

Paul wrote this:

> It is God's will that you should be sanctified: that you should avoid sexual immorality; that each of you should learn to control his own body in a way that is holy and honorable, not in passionate lust like the heathen, who do not know God; and that in this matter no one should wrong his brother or take advantage of him. The Lord will punish men for all such sins, as we have already told you and warned you. For God did not call us to be impure, but to live a holy life.
>
> —1 Thessalonians 4:3-7

Just a few sentences later in that same letter Paul wrote about the rapture of the church. It seems he almost had insight into the future knowing that one of Satan's final attacks against humanity would be an overwhelming deluge of filth called pornography, because the word "fornication" which is used in the King James translation of that passage comes from the Greek word, porneo, where we get our modern word "pornography." Fornication includes everything from lust to sex itself. It includes homosexuality, lesbianism, sex outside of marriage and lust incited by pornography.

How do bad sexual habits start? Isaiah 59 indicates that something is planted in the mind that conceives sin.

> They hatch the eggs of vipers and spin a spider's web. Whoever eats their eggs will die, and when one is broken, an adder is hatched.
>
> —Isaiah 59:5

There was a Hebrew saying that a rooster laid an egg, and the man who owned the rooster was full of lust, and when he gathered the eggs from the rooster and cracked one open, a deadly viper came out and bit him. That viper was called a cockatrice, or an evil snake, and its power was said to come when a person committed a sin with their eye, most probably sexual lust.

That is how pornography works: Satan plants snake eggs in poeple's minds every time they see those images, and sooner or later those eggs hatch and they are poisoned. There is a spirit behind pornography, and behind many less openly offensive programs or magazines, and that spirit plants the eggs as you indulge its sinful message.

One time my kids had friends over and they were watching a popular program, and I could tell there was a bad spirit behind it after watching it for only a few seconds. My own spirit was grieved at the sensuality and scorn for morality the characters showed.

Are They There?

Snake eggs can be planted in your mind apparently with no effect, and we can be fooled into thinking we are safe. But in truth they are incubating, and one day they will hatch. I have heard of horrible crimes committed by outwardly normal people who had for many years filled their minds with snake eggs.

One pornographic magazine ran an article about how to have a more powerful orgasm by tying a rope around your neck and choking off the air just before orgasm. Not long after that, people noticed that more teenaged boys were committing suicide. In reality, they had gotten this magazine and were trying to experience this rush and there was nobody to undo the rope when they passed out. The parents were often too embarrassed to tell people that their son died masturbating. I have experienced the painful task of conducting funerals for boys who died that way.

I talked with a young minister who ran up a phone bill of hundreds of dollars having homosexual fantasies — on his church line. He said his foray into homosexuality started with homosexual pornography, which led him to question his own sexuality. Christians are not immune from the onslaught. Many have minds full of snake eggs that will one day hatch if they are not taken care of.

Recently I have noticed a jarring trend in which a spouse will suddenly walk out of the marriage relationship, and in a week or so be living with someone else. I have sat in executive meetings dealing with people who have committed adultery or been caught with a prostitute, and in every instance the seeds of lust had been planted long before those seeds bore the fruit of adultry.

I was stunned when a lady I had known for years, one of the best church workers we had, left her husband and children and moved in with another man. When pressed on the issue, she said she had thought about it for ten years. She had incubated and nurtured snake eggs.

I have seen pictures of parasites that live in human beings, and they are the ugliest creatures imaginable. Some have club heads, others have beaks, and all of them look like hideous monsters — but they live inside of every human being. The only good thing is that they never grow big enough to kill us. Snake eggs are vastly more dangerous, and far uglier when they hatch. And yet some people are more concerned with outward cleanliness — getting rid of the bacteria and microbes on their bodies — than with getting rid of the spiritual and mental parasites breeding in their minds.

I heard a statistic that nearly all rapes and violent sexual crimes have roots in pornography. Mass murderer, Ted Bundy, confessed to Dr. James Dobson on video that his wicked ways began with so-called soft-core pornography. He began to think women were lower than men and should be dominated. The women he killed were the victims of hatched snake eggs.

When They Hatch

I have a friend who is a pastor, and his associate came to him one day and asked if he could borrow the communion cups for a Bible study he was holding. The pastor asked where the Bible study was, and the associate told him it was at a nudist resort. The pastor was horrified when the man told him what a liberating experience public nudity was! He was fired on the spot, and later the former associate's daughter came by the church and said, "My dad has been a creep ever since I can remember. He always had pornographic magazines around the house. When his friends would come over he would tell me to go to my room, and I would look out of my window and see them sitting naked in the back yard drinking coffee."

That man willingly bred and hatched snake eggs in his mind, and it cost him his job and the respect of his family. He thought social nudity would set him free. It is the Son of God that sets us free! Read through the New Testament and you will see that whenever people got naked in public, there was always demon possession involved. In Luke eight, a demon possessed man wore no clothes. In Acts 19:13, the sons of Sceva went to cast out a demon, and the demon stripped them and made them run naked from the house.

James 1:15 says that lust conceives and results in death. That death takes place over time, and joy drains out of your heart like oil from a leaky oil pan. Sometimes I see young unmarried couples coming to church, excited and happy, enjoying their courtship. Then they start sitting farther back and begin to look gloomy. I know what has happened. They have given in to lust and their joy is draining away.

I watched a news report about how kids are being taught in school that it's normal for boys to marry boys, and girls to marry girls, and for lesbians to be artificially inseminated so they can have babies. Those snake eggs of immorality are being laid in the minds of children even now in our public schools.

What To Do

If you have been ensnared and trapped it does not mean you are an evil person. It means you need some help getting out.

> Live by the Spirit, and you will not gratify the desires of the sinful nature. For the sinful nature desires what is contrary to the Spirit, and the Spirit what is contrary to the sinful nature. They are in conflict with each other, so that you do not do what you want. But if you are led by the Spirit, you are not under law.
>
> —Galatians 5:16-18

Number One: Recognize and confess our weaknesses to God and to one another.

If you have been tested, understand that everyone else has been, too. The body of Christ is here not to shoot you or slice you up with the sword of the Spirit, but to help you get those eggs out of your mind.

> If we confess our sins, he is faithful and just
> and will forgive us our sins and purify us from
> all unrighteousness.
>
> —1 John 1:9

When you have confessed your sins, you can be strong to take a stand against sexual temptation. I worked at a power company before I was in the ministry and one day a guy came by while I was sitting at my desk, and he had a picture of a naked woman. "What do you think about that?" he asked. I answered, "Give me a break. What do you have at home that would make you want to look at that low-class stuff? That is nothing but a hamburger compared to the steak I have at home." From that point on the public viewing of pornography went down because the other men did not want me to think they had ugly wives.

Number Two: Avoid lust-producing situations.

The Bible says:

> Flee the evil desires of youth, and pursue righteousness, faith, love and peace, along with those who call on the Lord out of a pure heart.
>
> —2 Timothy 2:22

> Flee from sexual immorality.
>
> —1 Corinthians 6:18a

> Avoid every kind of evil.
>
> —1 Thessalonians 5:22

Regaining Your Spiritual Momentum

The idea here is to actively avoid and run from any situation or location that would increase the likelihood of sinful behavior.

• Do not let R-rated movies into your home.

• Do not drive through parts of town where there are strip joints and X-rated shops.

• Do not read the part of the newspaper with the X-rated advertisements.

• Do not have cable television or a satellite system if you cannot avoid the X-rated channels.

• Do not walk near the desk of someone at work whom you find sexually attractive.

• Maintain a healthy sexual relationship with your spouse.

All of us can learn from this biblical, practical advice.

One time many years ago, I was in the Dallas airport bookstore when I noticed the girly magazines in the magazine rack. I started to get excited, and I thought, "I am in Dallas, nobody knows me here." I inched my way over to the magazines, and all the while my heart was racing. I wanted to take just one little peek, and I could not believe it was happening. One part of me was saying, "Do it!" and the other part was saying, "Jesus help me!" Before I touched a

132

magazine an announcement came over the loud speaker saying: "Billy Graham, please pick up the white courtesy telephone." That jolted me! I got out of there so fast I must have been a blur. I did not want to get caught by Billy Graham. All the way I was saying, "Thank you, Jesus! You made a way of escape."

We are told in First Corinthians 10:13 that there is no temptation that has faced you or me that has not faced others. And there is no temptation that you face that Jesus did not face Himself. He promised He would make a way of escape. If you look, it will be there.

Number Three: Rely on the Holy Spirit's power.

Breathe the Name of Jesus. In Luke, Jesus said:

> **I have given you authority to trample on snakes and scorpions and to overcome all the power of the enemy; nothing will harm you.**
>
> **—Luke 10:19**

We are supposed to be treading on the serpents, not letting them plant their eggs in us!

A friend of mine was in a hotel room one night and he turned on the television which was tuned into pornography. He watched five minutes of it, and after he shut it off he felt like there were a thousand little spiders all over his brain. He prayed for two and a half hours, and pictured Jesus sitting there picking each spider off.

Rely on the power of the Holy Spirit and, God help us, never let us be deceived into thinking we have a share in God's kingdom if we are committing the sins of pornography, or we may never find our way back onto the Road to Success.

Chapter Eleven

The Danger Of Drifting Away

Have you ever found yourself dozing off at the wheel? If so, you know the horror of opening your eyes to see that you have drifted across the line into opposing traffic, or onto the shoulder of the road.

Perhaps you have been deep in thought and drifted onto the wrong connecting highway, or forgotten to take the correct exit. Either way, drifting can cause harm, from delaying our arrival to causing premature death.

To drift is to miss the mark, to go forward without purpose or clear direction, to stray from the course. Even though revival is sweeping churches around the world, and many Christians are having times of wonderful spiritual experience, there is still great danger of drifting from the Road to Success.

A few years ago I was vacationing with my family. At a nearby lake we took inner tubes out on the water, swimming and having a great time. My inner tube was pretty comfortable, and after I was worn out from playing I decided to relax and close my eyes. The warm sun felt so good on my face, and the water cooled my back. It felt wonderful to let go for a while.

But when I woke up I felt weeds all around me, poking my hands and feet. I looked around and realized I had drifted across the lake into a marshy area. I quickly paddled toward our lake cabin, but even with great effort it took more than thirty minutes to reach it. I was alarmed at how quickly my surroundings had changed after I closed my eyes. Because of carelessness I could have been hit by a boat, sunk by a fisherman's hook, or stumbled on a nest of water snakes.

None of us should think we are immune from drifting. If you recall, one of the flags on the Road of Failure was self-confidence, or the belief that we cannot fail. It is possible for any Christian on the Road to Success to drift, and none of us should consider ourselves exempt from the lures of roadside attractions.

First Timothy 4:1 says that in the latter times some will depart from the faith. The indication is of a slow, subtle drift that includes giving heed to seducing spirits and doctrines of devils, speaking lies and hypocrisy, and having their consciences seared with a hot iron.

The Spirit clearly says that in later times some will abandon the faith and follow deceiving spirits and things taught by demons.

Proverbs 14:12 describes the backslider when it says:

> **There is a way that seems right to a man, but in the end it leads to death.**

Hebrews 6:4-6 says:

> **It is impossible for those who have once been enlightened, who have tasted the heavenly gift, who have shared in the Holy Spirit, who have tasted the goodness of the word of God and the powers of the coming age, if they fall away, to be brought back to repentance, because to their loss they are crucifying the Son of God all over again and subjecting him to public disgrace.**

I am always amazed when I hear about people who have drifted from God, who were once knowledgeable of the Word of God and seemed to have it all together. Step by step, inch by inch they took their eyes off the road and drifted away.

> **If we deliberately keep on sinning after we have received the knowledge of the truth, no sacrifice for sins is left, but only a fearful expectation of judgment and of raging fire that will consume the enemies of God.**
>
> **—Hebrews 10:26, 27**

Drifting can happen during catnaps like the one I took on the lake, and during spiritual catnaps when we say things like, "I don't need to go to church this week. I will just relax and watch a preacher on television." Or, "That thing is not really sin. I will go ahead and try a little bit, and if it angers God, I know He will forgive me."

Backsliding

Drifting is sometimes known by another word: Backsliding, a biblical word meaning to get off the right path and onto the road of apostasy. It does not mean that a man or woman has denied the Lord, but that he or she is moving in that direction. The Hebrew word for backsliding means to drift off target and wind up in a cage, like a wild animal.

When I was twenty-one years old I went to a tent meeting with two of my friends, Terry and Howard. I was not saved at the time, and that night the pastor preached a message from the book of Daniel. At the end of the sermon he asked how many would like to accept Jesus Christ as their Savior. Every head was bowed, every eye closed, and I thought surely everybody would raise their hands, so I lifted my hand. The next thing I knew people had surrounded me saying, "Praise the Lord, brother. We want to welcome you into the family." I thought, "Lord, You sure snuck me in, didn't You?" I did not know exactly what had happened, but I was a changed person. In the next few weeks I went to church as often as I could and soaked in the preaching. I was having all kinds of fun.

Then my friend Howard got married, and Terry was the best man. After the wedding, Terry drove Howard and his new wife to their hotel, and I was left with another Christian named Vince, who was the kind of guy who would lean over when the preacher was preaching and make some smart remark. He was always criticizing or murmuring. I should have known better than to hang around with him.

Vince and I were left together after the wedding and he said, "Dave, why don't we go down to the bar and have a beer to celebrate the wedding?" I was only a couple of months old in the Lord and I said, "Do you think that would be right?" He told me how Jesus turned water into wine, so I said, "What about being there with all of the drunks and sinners?" He told me how Jesus went out among the sinners, and was criticized by the religious leaders for it. Every argument he had sounded so logical, so finally I told him I would go with him, order a soda and witness to people.

I realize now I was like a mouse being hypnotized by a boa constrictor in a glass tank. We used to have a boa constrictor named Ben in my biology class in high school. We would put mice and frogs in his tank and Ben would hypnotize those little animals. First they would try to escape, but after a while they would wear themselves out, and then Ben would look right at the frog or the mouse and it was almost as if there was something intriguing in the snake's eyes, and the frog or mouse would stand completely still as Ben got closer and finally popped it into his mouth. I felt like I was in a cage with a boa constrictor and I was slowly being hypnotized, although I did not realize it.

We found ourselves in this bar and Vince started pressuring me to have a beer. Jesus drank wine, he told me, and Paul told Timothy to take a little wine for his stomach. Beer did not have as much alcohol as wine, he said, and finally I relented and ordered a beer, and oh, it tasted good, but I felt terribly guilty. To cover over the guilt I ordered another one and tried to convince myself that Vince was right, and the next thing I knew I was ordering hard liquors and we were singing "Jesus loves me, this I know for the Bible tells me so."

The next thing I remember is waking up with bright lights overhead, doctors and a chaplain standing over me, and blood everywhere. My head was smashed open, my chest was crushed, and I had no idea what had happened to me. I still don't know exactly, except that I had a car accident, and I spent several weeks in the hospital.

Do you think Vince called or sent me a get well card? No. But Terry and Howard, the guys who loved the Lord, did. They turned out to be my real friends.

I had drifted because of carelessness. Granted, I was a baby Christian, but I had let down my guard, and started to justify the sin that had lured me in. Vince had abused the grace of God, and convinced me to do the same, ignoring the cautions the Bible gives about turning the grace of God into lasciviousness.

I am still embarrassed to tell that story, but it is a good example of how easily we can drift, even when we sincerely love the Lord.

Two Types Of Christians

There are two kinds of Christians: Abraham Christians and Lot Christians. The Abraham kind live well, faithful and prepared. They walk in God's blessing and escape the world's destruction with their heavenly reward intact. Terry and Howard were this kind of Christian.

The Lot kind are different. They walk in difficulty and worldliness and barely escape with their lives. Vince was a Lot kind of Christian.

You may be familiar with the story of Lot and Abraham which led to the destruction of Sodom and Gomorrah. Let me summarize it briefly, and then show you the differences in character of these two men.

Lot was Abraham's nephew. When Lot's father died, Abraham took him under his wing and taught him God's ways. Lot was something of an understudy in Abraham's household, evidenced by the fact that he is mentioned specifically when Abraham left his father's household.

> So Abram departed as the LORD had instructed him, and Lot went with him. Abram was seventy-five years old when he left Haran. He took his wife, Sarai, his nephew Lot, and all his wealth — his livestock and all the people who had joined his household at Haran — and finally arrived in Canaan.
>
> —Genesis 12:4,5 (NLT)

Abraham and Lot both prospered and their flocks grew so large that they decided to split up to avoid fighting among their employees. Lot moved to a place near Sodom and Abraham stayed in Canaan. Their decisions from that point on show us the two different roads you and I can take in our walk with God.

Both men had equal opportunities with God, but as we shall see, one went a sad, hard way and the other went a way of blessing and reward.

Why? There are four answers:

1. They made different choices.

2. They took different directions.

3. They had different priorities.

4. They developed different lifestyles.

Choices

In Genesis eighteen, we read how God came to Abraham before He destroyed Sodom and Gomorrah. This tells us a lot about how Abraham had developed a relationship with God. They grew so close that God shared His plans with Abraham in advance. The Lord said to Himself:

> "Should I hide my plan from Abraham?" the LORD asked. "For Abraham will become a great and mighty nation, and all the nations of the earth will be blessed through him."
>
> —Genesis 18:17,18 (NLT)

The two cities, God said, were notoriously wicked, and needed to be eradicated because they dishonored Him and their sin might infect the rest of the world. Abraham, sensitive in heart, immediately interceded for the cities.

> Will you destroy innocent and guilty alike? Suppose you find fifty innocent people there within the city — will you still destroy it, and not spare it for their sakes? ... Should not the Judge of all the earth do what is right?
>
> —Genesis 18:23b-25b (NLT)

God listened to his request and agreed to not destroy the cities if He found only ten innocent people there. Abraham's sensitivity to the heart of God enabled him to make the request.

Lot, on the other hand, was so spiritually insensitive that when two angels visited his town, he thought they were men.

> That evening the two angels came to the entrance of the city of Sodom, and Lot was sitting there as they arrived. When he saw them, he stood up to meet them. Then he welcomed them and bowed low to the ground. "My lords," he said, "come to my home to wash your feet, and be my guests for the night. You may then get up in the morning as early as you like and be on your way again..."
>
> —Genesis 19:1, 2 (NLT)

When the homosexuals in that city came after the angels and tried to beat Lot's door down so they could rape them, Lot stood against them:

> "Please, my brothers," he begged, "don't do such a wicked thing."
>
> —Genesis 19:7 (NLT)

He had become like his surroundings, even calling those depraved sinners "brothers." Then, when the angels warned him of the judgment, he initially had a hard time comprehending it. Instead of fleeing immediately, he suggested delaying their escape. Finally, when he got the picture, he was unable to convince his sons-in-law to go with him, and they perished in the judgment. Lot's last hours there were frantic, desperate, disorganized, and panicked. The angels had to literally drag him out of the city with his wife and two daughters, and then he argued with the angels about where he should go.

Lot lost nearly everything in that escape. His wife was killed when she turned to look back at the cities; he lost sons-in-law, property, livelihood, everything but his daughters, and they had brought Sodom and Gomorrah with them in their hearts, as was evidenced later when they got their father drunk and slept with him to bear children.

What was Abraham doing all the while? Having fun with the Lord, going down the Road to Success.

Early on in the story, when it was time for Abraham and Lot and their herdsmen to split up, the two men stood at a high place overlooking the land and Abraham let Lot choose which part of the land he wanted. Lot looked out on the land with his natural eye. He was a believer, but he looked at the area near Sodom and thought how prosperous it appeared. Ambition for wealth and prestige took a higher place in his mind than did the will of God, and he neglected to take into consideration the moral standards of the people. He sought not the direction of the Lord and instead chose for himself the land near Sodom, not foreseeing the detrimental effect it would have on his spiritual life or family.

Every Christian will face a choice to serve God or money. Jesus said no one can serve two masters. If you serve God, the other things will be added unto you and you will gain both. If money is your priority, you will drift from God and lose His presence, and eventually give up your material riches, too.

Jesus faced this choice when the devil showed him all the kingdoms of the world and said, and I paraphrase, *If you worship me, all these things can be yours, Jesus. This shopping center over here, these skyscrapers, this expensive downtown property, this castle in Europe, this beach house in Maui. Think of the money and reputation you will have!* Jesus sternly responded, "Get behind me Satan for it is written, 'Thou shalt worship the Lord thy God and only the Lord thy God shalt thou worship'" (Luke 4:8 KJV).

Lot was looking for a city that would promote him financially, while Abraham was looking for a city whose maker was God. Lot found wealth in the world system, but gained a city made by human hands. He made the wrong choice and lost everything he'd worked for.

What choice do you make when you look upon the world's wealth? Do you lust after the high-rise apartments, the padded stock portfolio, the expensive SUV? Does this lust cloud your mind and affect your choices? If so, you are on the same road as Lot was. Keep in mind that only one city will be left standing at the end of the age — the one Abraham sought, the one I seek, the one true believers long for, the city at the end of the Road to Success whose builder is God.

Direction

Another difference between Lot and Abraham is the directions they took. Abraham followed God though he did not always understand the direction. Lot, on the other hand seemed to like directions that made sense to his human mind.

I remember reading about Pat Robertson, the President of the Christian Broadcasting Network. He graduated from an Ivy League school, and realized God had given him knowledge in business principles, so he went to New York to make his fortune in the stock market, but things did not work out the way he had planned. He decided that he and his wife would fast for seven days in their little New York apartment. At the end of the seven days the Lord said, "I want you to sell all your furniture and give it to the Lord. I want you to go to Virginia." They did not know what was going on, but they went to Virginia, and when they arrived with only seventy or so dollars in their pockets, God said, "I want you to buy that television station that is for sale."

They bought the station, which was not very impressive at the time. They had to pray over the antenna so that it would stay up. They had one camera and knew nothing about television and yet they were following the direction of the Lord.

Today most of us know the impact CBN has had around the world, all because Pat Robertson decided to be an Abraham-type of Christian.

Sad to say, Lot-type Christians are vastly more common than Abraham ones. They follow their own direction without seeking God. They do not fast and pray for direction, but use worldly wisdom, letting God be at best their fourth or fifth consideration. How different the world would be if there were more Abraham Christians! God could do so much more through willing people.

Priorities

Lot and Abraham had different priorities. Lot seemed to want fame and power on his own terms, and was willing to put his family in jeopardy to get them. He was able to avoid the gross temptations of his city, but did not realize that his children were weaker than he.

The Bible tells us in Second Peter, chapter two, that Lot's soul was vexed because of the wickedness around him. Vexed means worn down, and indicates that Lot let down his guard and developed a libertarian type of attitude that said, "I will let everyone else be the way they want to be. I won't interfere with them. I don't have any right to tell them what is wrong or right." He neglected the commission that comes with following God that we are to share God's laws and principles so people can have better lives. He had a "to-each-his-own" attitude.

Lot was promoted to mayor of the city. Some scholars say he was like a supreme court judge. He was moving up in worldly circles, but Abraham was moving closer to God. Their priorities were different. Abraham followed God's direction and built altars everywhere he went, proclaiming the Name of his God. Abraham's life was not without incident or problems. He made mistakes on many occasions, but his priority was to live for God. He was a soul winner, getting servants from other nations and teaching them about God. He trained them and made them disciples. We read about some of Abraham's servants who prayed for guidance while on a journey, and then gave thanks and praise to God when He graciously showed them the way.

Abraham talked with God as you or I would talk to another person. God valued his friendship because Abraham made God a priority. We never see God talking to Lot like He did to Abraham. In fact, Lot only escaped destruction because Abraham was an intercessor, which is one of the highest calling a believer can have. Intercession is the present day ministry of Jesus Christ; the Bible calls Christians a royal priesthood, and the main function of a priest is to intercede.

Abraham interceded for the nation and God listened to him because his priorities were in the right order.

Lifestyles

The people around Abraham were becoming more like Abraham, but Lot was becoming more like the people he was around. They chose completely different lifestyles. Abraham was wealthy, well-liked, a prince among those in the land. He had everything

Lot set his sights on, yet Abraham chose a godly lifestyle.

Different lifestyles lead to different outcomes. Lot lived in a spiritually polluted place, life with the diseases associated with homosexuality, and died broke, living in an old cave with two daughters who were given over to immorality. Lot's daughters gave birth to the Moabites and the Ammonites who became the greatest enemies of Israel.

Abraham's lifestyle led to a much better result. He lost nothing in the destruction of Sodom and Gomorrah. His son married a godly woman, and out of that line came the Messiah, Jesus Christ. Both Lot and Abraham escaped God's wrath, but one escaped with complete protection while the other barely made it. Why? Different choices, different directions, different priorities and different lifestyles.

Maybe someone you know has drifted from the faith. Maybe at one time you went down that road, too. What else can we learn about drifting, and why does it happen to people who know God? In the next chapter we will look at some of the most sinister causes of drifting, and how to avoid them.

If you seek to hold onto a temporal thing at the expense of an eternal thing, you are going to lose both!

Chapter Twelve

The Causes Of Drifting

I have observed over the years that there are four main reasons people drift.

First Cause of Drifting: Carelessness or compromise.

Samson was raised up and groomed by God to be the deliverer of Israel, but Samson was sloppy, undisciplined and careless. He should have been praying and doing everything he could to maintain his anointing of strength, but he spent his time playing riddles until one morning he made a serious mistake without realizing it. He had drifted outside the sphere of God's protection, like someone driving far out on a country road and running out of gas.

The enemy came to town to capture Samson, and Samson said, "No problem. I am the anointed of God, the deliverer of Israel. I will wipe out these enemies."

But his hair had been cut off, his strength was gone and the enemy captured Samson and gouged his eyes out.

That is one of the first things that happens to us when we drift from God. We lose our vision for our church, for our life, for lost souls. Then, like Samson, we become slaves to the enemy. It started with a touch of carelessness and compromise.

Second Cause of Drifting: Listening to faith-destroying teaching.

Imagine you are driving down God's highway and you pick up a hitchhiker, though that is not a good idea these days. He tells you, "This is not the road you want. It will not really work in getting you where you want to go. You may as well take another one." He fills the air with cynicism and clouds your view. The faith you once had that the road was the right one is now diminished.

That is what faith-destroying teaching is like.

There was a season early in my ministry when magazines were coming to our home from certain evangelists and ministries who attacked spiritual principles I believed in. This was when Mary Jo and I were standing on God's promises for nearly every provision in our lives, yet I was susceptible to negative teaching because I did not want to displease God in any way. After reading those negative magazines I prayed, "God, if it is wrong for me to claim this and that promise, I won't." I felt deflated because God's promises were all I had.

Mary Jo and I took a walk one evening and I asked if she thought God was speaking to us through the magazines. She said, "We need to get home in the living room, have a praise session and find out from God ourselves."

We went home that night, went into the living room and started praising the Lord. We did not feel like it, but we did it anyway, praising and dancing and lifting up His Name. Then we began to pray and ask all of our questions, and suddenly a holy silence came over the room and a voice as from beyond the stars penetrated my spirit and I spoke out the Word from the Lord: "Thus saith God, all Scripture is given by my inspiration and is profitable for you. Believe it and watch me perform it, saith the Lord."

There was rejoicing in my living room that night! We threw away all the faith-destroying junk we had received, and soon thereafter saw the continued faithfulness of God in our lives. We stood on His promises and saw them come to pass.

Paul wrote to Timothy:

> Cling tightly to your faith in Christ, and always keep your conscience clear. For some people have deliberately violated their consciences; as a result, their faith has been shipwrecked. Hymenaeus and Alexander are two examples of this. I turned them over to Satan so they would learn not to blaspheme God.
>
> —1 Timothy 1:19-20 (NLT)

Some people have allowed their lives to be shipwrecked because they have listened to Alexander and Hymenaeus types who tear down people's faith. If you lose faith, you lose power and you will be shipwrecked. As long as a ship maintains its power, it can cut through a storm. Don't listen to negative teaching.

Third Cause of Drifting: Letting the cares of life and personal ambitions get above the will of God.

It is easy to take back control of our career. Sometimes we go our own way and promise God we will give Him some air time by talking now and then about "the heavenly deity" or "supreme being" to our co-workers.

The Bible says, "He who seeks to keep his life will lose it, and he who will lose his life for Christ's sake will gain it" (Luke 9:24). If you seek to hold onto a temporal thing at the expense of an eternal thing, you are going to lose both, as Lot did.

This is what happened to Judas Iscariot. He did not start out to be a bad person, but a disciple of Christ — selected by Christ. There is no outward indication that Judas had drifted until the last year of Jesus' ministry on the earth. The first two and a half years, Judas was casting out devils, healing the sick. But his ambitions got the best of him. He wanted Jesus to lead a revolution and install Judas as a powerful adviser. When he saw that this was not going to happen, he made miscalculations. When he sold Jesus into the hands of his enemies for thirty pieces of silver, I do not believe he realized what he was doing. He probably thought they would whip Jesus and let Him go. He never knew that they would put Jesus on a cross to die, and indeed he took back the silver he had gained. He made a misjudgment. He had drifted so far that he did not foresee the consequences.

Fourth Cause of Drifting: Sin.

King Saul was an outstanding young man chosen by God to lead Israel, but he allowed sin to remain in his life. He did not obey God but followed his own ways, and drifted from the sphere of God's protection so badly that he ended up consulting a medium — a witch.

Every person needs direction and guidance. If we are not being directed by God, we are being directed by somebody else, like Saul's fortune teller, the witch of Endor. The last we hear of Saul is when he took his own sword and fell on it. The nation was in shock. Perhaps only Saul's close advisers knew he had drifted from his first love. Sin can cause us to drift unnoticeably until a crisis comes.

Augustine, the early Christian theologian, told of a friend who would never go to gladiator fights because they were so bloody. One day his friends forced him to go, but he kept his hand over his eyes. He heard an agonizing scream and opened his finger a little bit to look. There was a man being gouged to death, bleeding profusely, and Augustine's friend closed his eyes. During the next fight he opened his fingers a little bit more, and by the end of the day he was cheering with the rest of the crowd.

That is what sin is like. It causes an imperceptible drift until we give full-hearted approval to horrible behavior.

Inoculation

A few years ago a person from our church went to Africa and came back with malaria. One of her friends came back dead. Apparently, they were not protected with the proper vaccinations.

The next time I and others went to Africa we were very careful to take precautions against disease. The doctors told us to watch out for mosquitoes, stay away from certain places. Then they gave us several shots to inoculate us against exotic diseases. We felt like pin cushions coming out of that office! If I remember correctly we got shots for cholera, tetanus, typhoid, malaria, hepatitis and other things I had never heard of.

I began to wonder, was there some way to inoculate ourselves against drifting? We all know the natural tendency of man is to go away from God, and only a concentrated, consistent effort keeps us going in the right direction. I believe the answer is "yes," there are ways to protect ourselves from drifting. Pull up your shirt sleeve and get ready for these inoculations against drifting.

Shot Number One: Watch out for people who justify little sins.

The longer I live the more I am convinced that we need to be ruthless against sin.

> I say this because some godless people have wormed their way in among you, saying that God's forgiveness allows us to live immoral lives. The fate of such people was determined long ago, for they have turned against our only Master and Lord, Jesus Christ.
>
> —Jude 1:4 (NLT)

My acquaintance, Vince, was the kind of person who justified sin rather than fled from it. In a way he was calling Jesus his Savior but denying Jesus' lordship. There is no such thing in God's Word as an unconditional promise, and our part of the deal is to continue in the faith, and stop justifying sin and leading others astray. Jude verse three says to "contend for the faith," which is what we must do to inoculate ourselves against the disease of backsliding.

Shot Number Two: Avoid murmurers and complainers.

> I must remind you — and you know it well — that even though the Lord rescued the whole nation of Israel from Egypt, he later destroyed every one of those who did not remain faithful. And I remind you of the angels who did not stay within the limits of authority God gave them but left the place where they belonged. God has kept them chained in prisons of darkness, waiting for the day of judgment. And don't forget the cities of Sodom and Gomorrah and their neighboring towns, which were filled with sexual immorality and every kind of sexual perversion. Those cities were destroyed by fire and are a warning of the eternal fire that will punish all who are evil. Yet these false teachers, who claim authority from their dreams, live immoral lives, defy authority, and scoff at the power of the glorious ones.
>
> —Jude 5-8 (NLT)

Why were the children of Israel left to die in the desert? Murmuring and complaining and faithlessness.

> They grumbled in their tents and did not obey the LORD.

—Psalm 106:25

Jude warns us against those who "defy authority," like the angels who fell from Heaven, and the people of Sodom and Gomorrah.

Murmuring is one of the major symptoms of drifting. I received a letter one time from a man who wrote that he had left the church two years earlier for what he thought were justifiable reasons, but his life quickly became a mess. He drifted from church to church, then fell into serious sin for more than a year. Through God's grace he was delivered from it, but he remained very angry at God and began to suffer physical illness, depression and anxiety attacks that forced him to take a leave of absence from his job. Two years after he left the church, he came back and the Lord restored his heart, showing him how the murmurings and dissatisfaction had led him astray. The man is right with God, but he lost two years wandering in the desert.

Shot Number Three: Build your life on faith.

But you, dear friends, must continue to build
your lives on the foundation of your holy faith.

—Jude 20a (NLT)

The first cause of drifting and murmuring is often impatience. I have learned that a large part of faith is simply waiting on God to do what He has promised, rather than rushing ahead of Him and being dissatisfied with His schedule. By nature, I like to push forward, farther and faster, doing as much ministry as I can, but that is not always the right way.

I write down my prayers, keeping a record of requests I make to God. One of those requests I made on November 20 one year, I wrote, "Father, please grant to this servant an international ministry." My first invitation to speak overseas came on November 20, two years later. I am glad I waited in faith rather than striving in self-effort.

Shot Number Four: Pray in the Spirit.

Jude goes on to say:

… pray in the Holy Spirit.

—Jude 20

No believer should go through life without a regular, Spirit-filled prayer time and prayer language. This Spirit-to-spirit contact with God heightens our sensitivity to Him, increasing our sense of peace and well-being and our knowledge of what He wants us to do.

Shot Number Five: Keep yourself in the love of God.

Some believers think the Christian life is a John Wayne movie where the tough cowboy travels alone through the wilderness. How dangerous! Keeping ourselves in the love of God, as Jude exhorts us, means keeping in fellowship with other believers. After all, love must be shown and shared to be real.

I was at a wedding one time when I met a man who went to our church, but who I had not seen for a while. I shook his hand and told him I had not seen him in church, and he began to rattle off reasons left and right.

"I am married now and need to spend time with my family."

"I am building a business. After all, God calls us to work faithfully."

By the end of our conversation he had given at least fourteen reasons for not being at church! Each reason probably had some validity, but none of them were reason enough to keep him from the fellowship of believers. I have had people quote the Bible and say, "I don't need church anymore. I have the Holy Spirit, and have no need of man teaching me." But the Bible also says not to forsake the assembling of ourselves (Hebrews 10:25).

Shot Number Six: Look forward to Heaven.

> **Keep yourselves in God's love as you wait for the mercy of our Lord Jesus Christ to bring you to eternal life.**
>
> **—Jude 21**

This means simply to anticipate with great joy the home that God is preparing for us on the other side of this life. I cannot wait to splash around in the River of Life, to jump in Jesus' arms and have Him tell me, "Well done, good and faithful servant." There are so many things I am looking forward to in Heaven. How about you?

Finding The Way

What if you have drifted from the Road to Success? Here are three quick steps to finding your way back.

Number One: Remember from where you have fallen.

Jesus said:

Look how far you have fallen from your first love!

—Revelation 2:5a (NLT)

Remember when you were first saved? You rallied people to go witnessing in the streets. You came early to Sunday evening services to pray around the altars. You read the Bible faithfully out of pure desire.

Do you recall those days? Or has it been that long?

Number Two: Repent.

Turn around. Find the right road and head back to your first love, Jesus. He will not overlook a humble heart that admits, "I have drifted and strayed. Help!"

Jesus said in the above verse:

Turn back to me again...

—Revelation 2:5b (NLT)

Do not make the mistake of saying, "I have only drifted a little bit," even if that is true. Let God judge that. He overlooks the arrogant heart, but honors the humble one.

The Bible says, "Draw near to God and He will draw near to you." When you decide to find the right road again, God will give you what amounts to a personal police escort. He will drive in front of you, leading you to the right place.

Number Three: Do the first things over again.

I remember a time when I strayed from the Lord. It was the most awful time of my life. I ended up getting on my face before God and saying, "I do not care if I die, I have to be right with You." When you are desperate like that, you get back to the basics. You recognize what you recognized at the very beginning — that you need salvation.

Jesus said:

> **Turn back to me again and work as you did at first.**
>
> **—Revelation 2:5b (NLT)**

Do the first things that once were part of your life. Go back to those basics — to prayer, to thinking about Jesus all day, to reading the Bible, to coming to every church service you can.

If you don't, you may end up on an even worse road — The Reprobate Road.

Chapter Thirteen

The Reprobate Road

I do not like to dwell on the subject of this chapter because I find it so distasteful, and yet there are some Christians who get this far and need a warning to get back on the Road to Success. If I did not know some Christians who are on the Reprobate Road, I probably would not be convinced that it was a problem; but it is. I have seen it, and I want us to recognize the signposts on that road so we can leave it quickly.

> They profess that they know God; but in works they deny *him*, being abominable, and disobedient, and unto every good work reprobate.
>
> —Titus 1:16 (KJV)

There is a class of people who know God, but end up rejecting Him. They follow the steps to a reprobate mind. Reprobate in its mild form means "cast away, rejected, worthless or useless." It means that God comes to a point where He has to turn people over to utter worthlessness. When someone hits the Reprobate Road, they approach a destination where they will be lost without any hope of being saved.

The Signposts

There are stages to a reprobate mind; to becoming lost without hope. There are also signposts which are meant to turn us around. Thank God for them!

Romans 1:21-28 gives us these signposts:

> Yes, they knew God, but they wouldn't worship him as God or even give him thanks. And they began to think up foolish ideas of what God was like. The result was that their minds became dark and confused. Claiming to be wise, they became utter fools instead. And instead of worshiping the glorious, ever-living God, they worshiped idols made to look like mere people, or birds and animals and snakes. So God let them go ahead and do whatever shameful things their hearts desired. As a result, they did vile and degrading things with each other's bodies. Instead of believing what they knew was the truth about God, they deliberately chose to believe lies. So they worshiped the things God made but not the Creator himself, who is to be praised forever. Amen. That is why God abandoned them to their shameful desires. Even the women turned against the natural way to have sex and instead indulged in sex with each other. And the men, instead of having normal sexual relationships with women, burned with lust for each other. Men did shameful things with other men and, as a result, suffered within themselves the

penalty they so richly deserved. When they refused to acknowledge God, he abandoned them
to their evil minds and let them do things that
should never be done.

—Romans 1:21-28 (NLT)

Signpost One: Not glorifying God.

Verse 21a says they knew God but would not worship Him as God.

Everybody has a God. The atheist has a god —
his belief that there is no god. He worships that belief. Everybody worships something because humans
were made with a longing in our hearts to worship.

If you refuse to listen to the LORD your God
and to obey the commands and laws he has
given you, all these curses will pursue and over-
take you until you are destroyed. These horrors
will serve as a sign and warning among you and
your descendants forever. Because you have not
served the LORD your God with joy and enthu-
siasm for the abundant benefits you have received, you will serve your enemies whom the
LORD will send against you.

—Deuteronomy 28:45-48a (NLT)

How would you like curses to literally chase you
around, like a Halloween witch on her broom? What
an awful thought!

How do we know if we are glorifying God? It boils
down to this: when faced with a conflict of interest,
what do you do?

a. Do you change yourself to line up with God's interest, like Abraham did?

b. Do you try to change God to line up with your interests, like Lot did?

If you do not glorify God with your choice, it leads to a second signpost.

Signpost Two: Not being thankful.

Verse 21b says the next step is not being thankful. Thankfulness and unthankfulness are developed traits. The same circumstances in two different lives can produce different results. There have been so many times God has stopped me from going in a direction, and at first I wondered why. Was He putting me on hold? It is easy to be unthankful when God's will conflicts with ours, but in the course of time I usually saw why His way was much better than mine.

Tough times will breed thankfulness or unthankfulness, depending on what your heart is made out of. The same sun that melts wax hardens clay.

Paul reminded believers that lack of thankfulness caused God to send a destroying angel to wreak havoc on the children of Israel.

> And don't grumble as some of them did, for that
> is why God sent his angel of death to destroy
> them.

—1 Corinthians 10:10 (NLT)

Are you thankful today? Everybody has a choice.
Habakkuk was a man who had received promises
from God, but there came a day when He wondered
if those promises were going to happen. He said:

> Even though the fig trees have no blossoms, and
> there are no grapes on the vine; even though the
> olive crop fails, and the fields lie empty and
> barren; even though the flocks die in the fields,
> and the cattle barns are empty, yet I will rejoice
> in the LORD! I will be joyful in the God of my
> salvation.

—Habakkuk 3:17, 18 (NLT)

Thanking God when there is no evidence is a sign
of strong faith. Unthankfulness becomes a god of
delusion, and leads directly to the next signpost.
There is no standing still on the Reprobate Road. It
is like a moving sidewalk.

Signpost Three: Having worthless imaginations.

Paul called it "foolish thoughts" or "vain and
empty" imaginations. On the Reprobate Road,
people eventually become worthless in their imaginations. The imagination in the Bible seems to be a
bridge between the mind and the spirit. It is neither

good nor evil, but is simply a tool that God has given us. You can use your imagination to worship God. You can picture yourself in the family room of Heaven with the Father inviting you up to His lap. I call that having faith movies, encouraging hope and positive visions to fill our minds; but when the faith movies become empty and vain, it means they are not according to God's script. They are vain and empty.

Satan has counterfeited the imagination in a thousand ways, but God intends us to battle back with right imaginations. If we don't, we reach the next signpost.

Signpost Four: A darkened heart.

Paul says their hearts became darkened and confused. Gradually, darkness replaces the light you once had. The Greek suggests that it means to lose the ability to see connections and consequences. Somebody asked me how ministers can fall away from God, and I replied that it is the same way anybody else does: progressively, step by step. The decision is never sudden. I have never seen anybody fall away from God instantaneously. Darkness sets like the sun, over time.

Going further down the Reprobate Road causes you to lose the ability to understand God's dealing in your life and to discern that which is of the devil and that which is of God. A darkened heart loses its awareness of God's presence. There are some people in the church who have lost the sense of the awareness of God's presence, and they think everyone else has, too. When we are close to God we maintain an awareness of His presence, whether our circumstances are good or bad, whether we feel like laughing or crying.

But when a heart is darkened, it loses the light of God's wisdom and a person begins to honor their own wisdom. The Bible says that all the treasures of wisdom are hidden in Christ Jesus. God's wisdom was to send His son to die on the cross and shed His blood for sin, bringing many into the family of God. Some discard that wisdom and claim there are many ways to God. In that moment, they become a fool. Others say Heaven and hell are right here on earth, and we can make our life one or the other. That, too, is foolishness because it goes against what the Bible tells us.

I was talking with an influential person one time, trying to convince her of her need for Jesus. She believed that if she lived a good enough life, she would go to Heaven. I asked what she expected to happen when she stood before God on judgment day, and she said, "He will have to understand that I tried my best."

She was professing a wisdom "superior" to God's.

I met a man in downtown Lansing where I was passing out Christian magazines, and he said, "I used to believe this stuff. I was in campus ministry. I believed in creation and all of that stuff until I went to the university and was enlightened. Now creation looks so foolish to me." He began to explain why evolution was true, and became frustrated with me when I told him I did not buy it. I did not possess the elite wisdom that he had. I believed then, as now, that all the wisdom and knowledge anyone needs are hidden in Christ Jesus — much more than we could comprehend. Any wisdom, philosophy, religion or teaching that does not line up with it is foolishness. The word "fools" in the Greek means "morons." When Paul says, "professing themselves to be wise, they became fools," he means they became, in modern terminology, morons. Paul had no patience for false wisdom.

You have heard the story just as I have. There once was a King who wanted a new suit of clothes, and along came two traveling tailors who said they had a new kind of material that only the wise could see, and they held up nothing. The King, not wanting to be thought a fool, agreed that the material was beautiful. Then he called in his counselors, and they too agreed that the material was worthy of a king, so the tailors were commissioned to make the King a new set of royal garments. They pretended to work the fabric, smoothing it out, sewing it, until finally the garment was ready. The King ordered that a great parade be held, and when he came through the town wearing only his underwear, none of the onlookers wanted to appear stupid so they told each other, "Isn't that suit beautiful?" But a little boy was perplexed and began to say, "The King has no clothes!" Soon everyone realized the truth and the King returned to the castle humiliated.

The point is that not all "wisdom" is wise. Other religions can seem flashy or intelligent or spiritual, but they offer a wisdom not of God.

Another way a person can honor their own wisdom over God's is to believe they can come to Christ anytime they want to, living a life of sin and degradation and making it right before they die. That is a form of trickery, not true repentance. When a person makes it right with God there is godly sorrow. It is not wise to wait. If you do, you may reach the next signpost.

Signpost Five: Becoming a humanist.

People try to de-dignify God and drag Him to the level of corruptible man so they can justify their sin. Romans 1:23 (KJV) says they "changed the glory [or the dignity] of the incorruptible God into an image made like to corruptible man." Then they digressed further and made gods in the form of birds, animals and reptiles. Humanism tries to elevate man to the position of God, and drag God to the level of His own creation.

Signpost Six: Calling God's truth a lie.

Why would anyone want to take God's glorious truth that sets people free and twist it into a lie? Simply this: They would rather twist the Word of God to accommodate their lifestyle rather than change their lifestyle to get into harmony with God.

Our culture is full of satisfied sinners. They do not want to change, and their lifestyle says, in essence, "God, you have lied." Then they reach the next signpost.

Signpost Seven: Worshiping created beings.

You can go into some young people's bedrooms and see who they adore the most by the posters plastered all over the walls. When Elvis Presley died, frenzied crowds of people almost worshiped the dead body of their king. When music or movie stars die today, fans grieve in such a way that it borders on worship.

It does not happen just when people die. We idolize people every day, whether a movie star, a spouse or a preacher. It is part of de-dignifying God, and it leads to the next signpost.

Signpost Eight: Serving the creature more than the Creator.

This signpost is subtle, but important. It appeals to human needs but neglects God's needs.

Jesus taught that we need to be concerned with serving mankind, but our service to mankind should grow out of our service to our Father in Heaven. Many humanitarian causes seem very worthy, but have at their core a desire to serve humanity before serving God. It is often difficult to see that this is a form of service that God does not accept, because anything that goes before our service to Him is wrong. The anti-Christ will be such a man. He will seem so benevolent and kind, but will lead people into the most extreme form of humanism and creature worship. It can start with a form of service that gives the appearance of nobility, but does not honor God.

Signpost Nine: Tolerating flagrant sin in other people.

The law-abiding people of Sodom and Gomorrah were judged along with the homosexuals because they tolerated sin in their midst.

If you tolerate sin in your family, God will judge you. I have seen families wracked and torn because parents did not stop their child's evil behavior, and everyone involved paid a high price. If you have the power to stop sin and you refuse to, God will judge you, and you will be one step closer to the final signpost.

Signpost Ten: Lost without hope.

> God gave them over to a reprobate mind, to do those things which are not convenient;
>
> —Romans 1:28b

God only knows how much time there is between signposts number one and ten, but there comes a point when God turns a person over to a reprobate mind, meaning they are beyond His reach. At this point God stops striving on your behalf and lets you go your own way. I imagine that of all the signposts, this is the most difficult to see because our blindness would be nearly complete.

This is a sobering truth, but there is hope. We can put the car in reverse and head back onto the main road before we reach the point of no return. Jesus said:

> **All that the Father gives me will come to me, and whoever comes to me I will never drive away.**
>
> —John 6:37

I don't know if I have ever met someone who was totally reprobate. Even those who swear against God can retain a desire to know Him, even if that desire is frustrated at times, but none of us should abuse God's grace and purposely put ourselves on the Reprobate Road, or the signposts may become difficult to recognize.

We all need to routinely assess which road we are on.

The Last Word

The humbling truth is that none of us started on the Road to Success, but Jesus found each of us in a ditch somewhere, or speeding down the Road to Failure, or off at a wrong exit. Not even the most virtuous Christian can credit superior driving skills or navigation techniques for where they are today.

We all need to routinely assess which road we are on. In this book we have talked about:

• The Road of Trouble, which all of us find ourselves on from time to time.

• Untangling other people's troubles, which helps us get off the Road of Trouble.

• Regaining our spiritual momentum after running out of gas, being weary at the wheel or driving while damaged.

You Can Have A New Start

God's forgiveness, acceptance, and power are available to you right now, no strings attached, just for the asking.

Just come to Jesus as you are (Romans 3:23). Admit your helplessness to save yourself (Romans 6:23, Luke 18:13). Ask Jesus to be your Saviour and to give you a new start (2 Corinthians 5:17), and confess with your mouth that He is Lord (Romans 10:9).

Why not pray this prayer right now? It will lead you to a brand new life. It is called a simple prayer of salvation:

> *Dear God,*
>
> *I come to you in the Name of Jesus. Your Word says in John 6:37 that if I turn to You, You will in no way cast me out, but You will take me in just as I am. I thank You, God, for that.*
>
> *You also said in Romans 10:13, that if I call upon You, I'll be saved. I'm calling on You, Lord, so I know You have now saved me.*
>
> *I believe Jesus died on the cross for me, and that He was raised from the dead. I now have a new life. My sins are gone, and I have a new start in life, beginning now! Thank You, Lord!*
>
> *Amen.*

If you prayed this prayer, call us at (517) 321-CARE and ask for your free book, *The New Life - The Start of Something Wonderful.* God Bless You!

About The Author

Dave Williams is pastor of Mount Hope Church and International Outreach Ministries, with world headquarters in Lansing, Michigan. He has served for over 20 years, leading the church in Lansing from 226 to over 4000 today. Dave sends trained ministers into unreached cities to establish disciple-making churches, and, as a result, today has "branch" churches in the United States, Philippines, and in Africa.

Dave is the founder and president of Mount Hope Bible Training Institute, a fully accredited institute for training ministers and lay people for the work of the ministry. He has authored 45 books including the fifteen-time best seller, *The Start of Something Wonderful* (with over 2,000,000 books sold), and more recently, *The Miracle Results of Fasting*, and *The Road To Radical Riches.*

The Pacesetter's Path telecast is Dave's weekly television program seen over a syndicated network of secular stations, and nationally over the Sky Angel satellite system. Dave has produced over 125 audio cassette programs including the nationally acclaimed *School of Pacesetting Leadership* which is being used as a training program in churches around the United States, and in Bible Schools in South Africa and the Philippines. He is a popular speaker at conferences, seminars, and conventions. His speaking ministry has taken him across America, Africa, Europe, Asia, and other parts of the world.

Along with his wife, Mary Jo, Dave established The Dave and Mary Jo Williams Charitable Mission (Strategic Global Mission), a mission's ministry for providing scholarships to pioneer pastors and grants to inner-city children's ministries.

Dave's articles and reviews have appeared in national magazines such as *Advance, The Pentecostal Evangel, Ministries Today, The Lansing Magazine, The Detroit Free Press* and others. Dave, as a private pilot, flies for fun. He is married, has two grown children, and lives in Delta Township, Michigan.

You may write to Pastor Dave Williams:

P.O. Box 80825

Lansing, MI 48908-0825

Please include your special prayer requests when you write, or you may call the Mount Hope Global Prayer Center anytime: (517) 327-PRAY

DECAPOLIS
PUBLISHING

For a catalog of products, call:

1-517-321-2780 or

1-800-888-7284

or visit us on the web at:

www.mounthopechurch.org

For Your Spiritual Growth

Here's the help you need for your spiritual journey. These books will encourage you, and give you guidance as you seek to draw close to Jesus and learn of Him. Prepare yourself for fantastic growth!

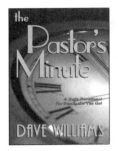

QUESTIONS I HAVE ANSWERED
Get answers to many of the questions you've always wanted to ask a pastor!

THE PASTOR'S MINUTE
A daily devotional for people on the go! Powerful topics will help you grow even when you're in a hurry.

ANGELS: THEY'RE WATCHING YOU!
The Bible tells more than you might think about these powerful beings.

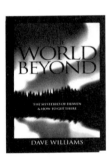

THE WORLD BEYOND
What will Heaven be like? What happens there? Will we see relatives who have gone before us? Who *REALLY* goes to Heaven?

FILLED!
Learn how you can be filled with the mightiest power in the universe. Find out what could be missing from your life.

STRATEGIC GLOBAL MISSION
Read touching stories about God's plan for accelerating the Gospel globally through reaching children and training pastors.

For Your Spiritual Growth

Here's the help you need for your spiritual journey. These books will encourage you, and give you guidance as you seek to draw close to Jesus and learn of Him. Prepare yourself for fantastic growth!

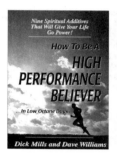

HOW TO BE A HIGH PERFORMANCE BELIEVER
Pour in the nine spiritual additives for real power in your Christian life.

SECRET OF POWER WITH GOD
Tap into the real power with God; the power of prayer. It will change your life!

THE NEW LIFE ...
You can get off to a great start on your exciting life with Jesus! Prepare for something wonderful.

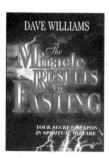

MIRACLE RESULTS OF FASTING
You can receive MIRACLE benefits, spiritually and physically, with this practical Christian discipline.

WHAT TO DO IF YOU MISS THE RAPTURE
If you miss the Rapture, there may still be hope, but you need to follow these clear survival tactics.

THE AIDS PLAGUE
Is there hope? Yes, but only Jesus can bring a total and lasting cure to AIDS.

These and other books available from Dave Williams and:

DECAPOLIS PUBLISHING

For Your Spiritual Growth

Here's the help you need for your spiritual journey. These books will encourage you, and give you guidance as you seek to draw close to Jesus and learn of Him. Prepare yourself for fantastic growth!

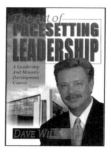

THE ART OF PACESETTING LEADERSHIP
You can become a successful leader with this proven leadership development course.

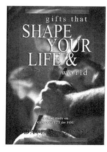

GIFTS THAT SHAPE YOUR LIFE
Learn which ministry best fits you, and discover your God-given personality gifts, as well as the gifts of others.

GROWING UP IN OUR FATHER'S FAMILY
You can have a family relationship with your heavenly father. Learn how God cares for you.

SUPERNATURAL SOULWINNING
How will we reach our family, friends, and neighbors in this short time before Christ's return?

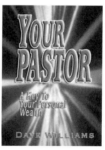

YOUR PASTOR: A KEY TO YOUR PERSONAL WEALTH
By honoring your pastor you can actually be setting yourself up for a financial blessing from God!

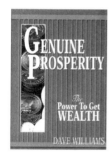

GENUINE PROSPERITY
Learn what it means to be truly prosperous! God gives us the power to get wealth!

These and other books available from Dave Williams and:

DECAPOLIS PUBLISHING

For Your Spiritual Growth

Here's the help you need for your spiritual journey. These books will encourage you, and give you guidance as you seek to draw close to Jesus and learn of Him. Prepare yourself for fantastic growth!

SOMEBODY OUT THERE NEEDS YOU
Along with the gift of salvation comes the great privilege of spreading the gospel of Jesus Christ.

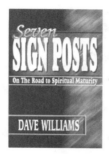

SEVEN SIGNPOSTS TO SPIRITUAL MATURITY
Examine your life to see where you are on the road to spiritual maturity.

THE PASTORS PAY
How much is your pastor worth? Who should set his pay? Discover the scriptural guidelines for paying your pastor.

DECEPTION, DELUSION & DESTRUCTION
Recognize spiritual deception and unmask spiritual blindness.

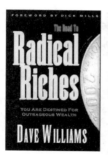

THE ROAD TO RADICAL RICHES
Are you ready to jump from "barely getting by" to Gods plan for putting you on the road to Radical Riches?

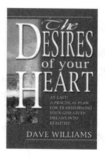

THE DESIRES OF YOUR HEART
Yes, Jesus wants to give you the desires of your heart, and make them realities.

These and other books available from Dave Williams and:

DECAPOLIS
PUBLISHING

For Your Successful Life

These video cassettes will give you successful principles to apply to your whole life. Each a different topic, and each a fantastic teaching of how living by God's Word can give you total success!

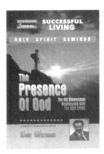

THE PRESENCE OF GOD
Find out how you can have a more dynamic relationship with the Holy Spirit.

FILLED WITH THE HOLY SPIRIT
You can rejoice and share with others in this wonderful experience of God.

GIFTS THAT CHANGE YOUR WORLD
Learn which ministry best fits you, and discover your God-given personality gifts, as well as the gifts of others.

THE SCHOOL OF PACESETTING LEADERSHIP
Leaders are made, not born. You can become a successful leader with this proven leadership development course.

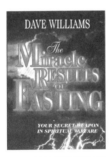

MIRACLE RESULTS OF FASTING
Fasting is your secret weapon in spiritual warfare. Learn how you'll benefit spiritually and physically! Six video messages.

A SPECIAL LADY
If you feel used and abused, this video will show you how you really are in the eyes of Jesus. You are special!

These and other videos available from Dave Williams and:

DECAPOLIS PUBLISHING

For Your Successful Life

These video cassettes will give you successful principles to apply to your whole life. Each a different topic, and each a fantastic teaching of how living by God's Word can give you total success!

HOW TO BE A HIGH PERFORMANCE BELIEVER
Pour in the nine spiritual additives for real power in your Christian life.

THE UGLY WORMS OF JUDGMENT
Recognizing the decay of judgment in your life is your first step back into God's fullness.

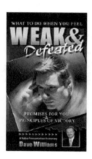

WHAT TO DO WHEN YOU FEEL WEAK AND DEFEATED
Learn about God's plan to bring you out of defeat and into His principles of victory!

WHY SOME ARE NOT HEALED
Discover the obstacles that hold people back from receiving their miracle and how God can help them receive the very best!

BREAKING THE POWER OF POVERTY
The principality of mammon will try to keep you in poverty. Put God FIRST and watch Him bring you into a wealthy place.

HERBS FOR HEALTH
A look at the concerns and fears of modern medicine. Learn the correct ways to open the doors to your healing.

These and other videos available from Dave Williams and:

DECAPOLIS PUBLISHING

Running Your Race

These simple but powerful audio cassette singles will help give you the edge you need. Run your race to win!

LONELY IN THE MIDST OF A CROWD
Loneliness is a devastating disease. Learn how to trust and count on others to help.

HERBS FOR HEALTH
A look at the concerns and fears of modern medicine. Learn the correct ways to open the doors to your healing.

HOW TO GET ANYTHING YOU WANT
You can learn the way to get anything you want from God!

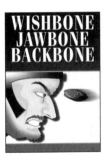

WISHBONE, JAWBONE, BACKBONE
Learn about King David, and how his three "bones" for success can help you in your life quest.

FATAL ENTICEMENTS
Learn how you can avoid the vice-like grip of sin and it's fatal enticements that hold people captive.

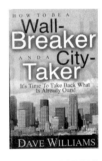

HOW TO BE A WALL BREAKER AND A CITY TAKER
You can be a powerful force for advancing the Kingdom of Jesus Christ!

These and other audio tapes available from Dave Williams and:

DECAPOLIS PUBLISHING

Expanding Your Faith

These exciting audio teaching series will help
you to grow and mature in your walk with Christ.
Get ready for amazing new adventures in faith!

THE BLESSING
Explore the many ways
that God can use you to
bless others, and how
He can correct the
missed blessing.

SIN'S GRIP
Learn how you can avoid
the vice-like grip of sin and
it's fatal enticements that
hold people captive.

FAITH, HOPE, & LOVE
Listen and let these three
"most important things in
life" change you.

**PSALM 91
THE PROMISE OF
PROTECTION**
Everyone is looking for
protection in these perilous
times. God promises
protection for those who
rest in Him.

**DEVELOPING
THE SPIRIT OF A
CONQUEROR**
You can be a conqueror
through Christ! Also, find
out how to *keep* those
things that you have
conquered.

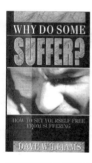

WHY DO SOME SUFFER
Find out why some people
seem to have suffering in
their lives, and find out
how to avoid it in your life.

Expanding Your Faith

These exciting audio teaching series will help you to grow and mature in your walk with Christ. Get ready for amazing new adventures in faith!

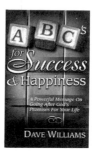

ABCs OF SUCCESS AND HAPPINESS
Learn how to go after God's promises for your life. Happiness and success can be yours today!

FORGIVENESS
The miracle remedy for many of life's problems is found in this basic key for living.

UNTANGLING YOUR TROUBLES
You can be a "trouble untangler" with the help of Jesus!

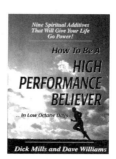

HOW TO BE A HIGH PERFORMANCE BELIEVER
Put in the nine spiritual additives to help run your race and get the prize!

BEING A DISCIPLE AND MAKING DISCIPLES
You can learn to be a "disciple maker" to almost anyone.

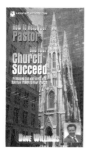

HOW TO HELP YOUR PASTOR & CHURCH SUCCEED
You can be an integral part of your church's & pastor's success.

These and other audio tapes available from Dave Williams and:

DECAPOLIS PUBLISHING

To order this
best-selling book
by Pastor Dave Williams,
mail this form with
payment to:

THE HOPE STORE
202 South Creyts Road
Lansing, Michigan 48917-9284

or:

PHONE
517-321-2780
800-888-7284

FAX
517-321-6332

WRITE
202 S. Creyts Rd.
Lansing, MI 48917

Please enter my order as follows:

☐ NEW LIFE (English)
☐ LA NUEVA VIDA (Spanish)

2-25	_____	@1.95 ea. _____
26-49	_____	@1.70 ea. _____
50-99	_____	@1.50 ea. _____
100-199	_____	@1.25 ea. _____
200-349	_____	@1.10 ea. _____
350-499	_____	@.95 ea. _____
500+	_____	@.75 ea. _____

Add 10% shipping/handling US _____
(15% shipping/handling Canada)
TOTAL INCLUDED WITH ORDER _____

Name _____

Business/Church _____

Address _____

City _____ State _____ ZIP _____

Telephone (_____) _____

Mastercard ☐   Visa ☐   (see below for ordering by credit card)

Authorized Signature _____

PLEASE SEND ME: One Case (150 books) of

☐ NEW LIFE (English)   ☐ LA NUEVA VIDA (Spanish)
   at the SPECIAL price of $142.50 per box **US** and $169.50 **CAN**
   (plus shipping — 10% US — 15% Canada)

MAIL ALL ORDERS TO: THE HOPE STORE
202 S. Creyts Rd. Lansing, MI 48917-9284

VISA/MASTERCARD ORDERS: Call 1-800-888-7284